Heart, Soul, Mind, and Strength

Also by Lynne Sandsberry

Good Chats:
Guided and Open Oral Discourse
For Advanced Students of English
(Bookman Books, Ltd., Taiwan)

Heart, Soul, Mind, and Strength

A Devotional on the Two Great Commandments

Lynne Sandsberry

WestBow
PRESS
A DIVISION OF THOMAS NELSON

Copyright © 2011 Lynne Sandsberry

All rights reserved. No part of this book may be used or reproduced by any means, graphic, electronic, or mechanical, including photocopying, recording, taping or by any information storage retrieval system without the written permission of the publisher except in the case of brief quotations embodied in critical articles and reviews.

WestBow Press books may be ordered through booksellers or by contacting:

WestBow Press
A Division of Thomas Nelson
1663 Liberty Drive
Bloomington, IN 47403
www.westbowpress.com
1-(866) 928-1240

Because of the dynamic nature of the Internet, any web addresses or links contained in this book may have changed since publication and may no longer be valid. The views expressed in this work are solely those of the author and do not necessarily reflect the views of the publisher, and the publisher hereby disclaims any responsibility for them.

Any people depicted in stock imagery provided by Thinkstock are models, and such images are being used for illustrative purposes only.

Certain stock imagery © Thinkstock.

ISBN: 978-1-4497-2257-9 (e)
ISBN: 978-1-4497-2258-6 (sc)
ISBN: 978-1-4497-2259-3 (hc)

Library of Congress Control Number: 2011914065

Printed in the United States of America

WestBow Press rev. date: 8/24/2011

Unless otherwise noted, Scripture quotations are taken from the New American Standard Bible, Copyright 1960, 1962, 1963, 1968, 1971, 1972, 1973, 1975, 1977, 1995 by The Lockman Foundation. Used by permission.

Scripture quotations noted NIV are taken from the Holy Bible, New International Version. Copyright 1973, 1978, 1984 by International Bible Society. Used by permission of Zondervan Publishing House. All rights reserved.

Scripture quotations noted KJV are taken from the King James Version of the Holy Bible.

To the One who created the eagle

and to my mother,

who has found great joy in sighting
eagles, owls, dippers, and "hummers"
all over God's earth

"Let's face it. Modern culture is not going to give us the time we need to develop a relationship with God. So we confront a choice. We cannot hope for support, but it is important that we know what we are up against and what's at stake. To take time in one's day for prayer and Bible reading is an anachronism in modern culture. It has about the same professional status as an ambition to become a career shepherd. But at least we know where we are. Support and understanding are out, but the still center is a priority all the same."[1]

Rebecca Manley Pippert[1]

Acknowledgments

I am deeply grateful to the Lord for the experience of composing these devotional readings. Using God-given gifts to write about God was as different from my usual writing tasks as wine is different from water. Before it was finished, I recognized that the book would always be as much for me as for future readers. God was already using individual readings to remind me of lessons I'll be reviewing for the rest of my life.

This devotional was written for the family of God, but in a sense it was also brought forth *by* the family. It was the point person; I authored the book. But many precious Christians—youth leaders, pastors, mentors, faithful friends—contributed to the "authoring" of the author, modeling their faith and God's great love. While the little pile of individual readings was slowly growing, dozens of Christians prayed for me and for the project. Other Christians I'd never met gave warm encouragement and permission to quote their materials. My coworker Grace Chen got me set up to type the manuscript; Echo Wei, Mary Chang, and Ingrid Chao took on computer tasks that saved me much time and stress; many others let me drag them from their lunch breaks for five-minute "fixes." My friend and colleague David Ludwig edited the completed manuscript as a gift. And the staff at WestBow ensured that the final product was sufficiently lovely and worthy to present to the rest of the family.

Thank you all.

Lynne Sandsberry
Taipei, 2011

Introduction

God's best gift arrived in Bethlehem some 2000 years ago, "a Savior who is Christ the Lord." The angels called it an event "of great joy which shall be for all the people." Merry Christmas to us, to all of us!

However, God's *first* gift to each of us was life itself. He gave us ourselves, made in His image, the pinnacle of His creation. He gave us minds capable of acquiring complex languages from infancy and using them to record knowledge and history; minds that can unravel the physical mysteries of the universe and produce feats of engineering and halt diseases. He gave us souls that delight in arrangements of color and shape and sound and smell and texture and taste, and the ability to mimic and recreate these in everything from art, poetry, and music to beauty products and food preparation. He gave us bodies with powerful maintenance systems, and the strength of heart and will that has allowed people to endure weeks and months of deprivation in times of wars and other disasters; that has enabled some people to choose a long and arduous path, or a deadly dangerous one, for the sake of a goal they deemed worthy, sometimes for the sake of people they didn't know.

Does God ask anything of us, beyond glad acceptance of His two wonderful gifts? When Jesus was asked to name the greatest commandment, he quoted Moses' words recorded in the Old Testament book of Deuteronomy:

"The foremost is, 'Hear, O Israel! The Lord our God is one Lord; and you shall love the Lord your God with all your heart, and with all your soul, and with all your mind, and with all your strength.' The second is this, 'You shall love your neighbor as yourself.' There is no other commandment greater than these" (Mark 12:29-31). On another occasion, Jesus added, "On these two commandments depend the whole Law and the Prophets" (Matt. 22:40).

This book is a daily devotional (142 readings) focused on our response to these commandments. May the words of scripture and the Spirit of Truth lead you day by day into a deeper love of God.

1

> One thing I do: forgetting what lies behind and reaching forward to what lies ahead, I press toward the goal for the prize of the upward call of God in Christ Jesus. Let us, therefore, as many as are perfect, have this attitude . . . . (Phil. 3:13-15)

A sportsman on a sailing race across the Atlantic Ocean had equipment failures and setbacks due to storm damage. When it was clear that he was so far behind the frontrunners that he had lost the chance to win an award, he became despondent. But then he gave himself a stern lecture. He remembered that many individual and corporate sponsors had invested money in his boat and in this undertaking, and he owed them, as he put it, "value for money." With that self-encouragement, he decided to once again put his full energies—heart, soul, mind, and strength, one might say—into sailing the best and fastest race possible.

Like the sportsman, we're in a kind of race, a sort of long-distance marathon. We're certainly running for ourselves, but not only for ourselves. Just as the sportsman would never have had a high-powered vessel to set in the water without his sponsors, so we run our race entirely by the grace of God. He provided us these phenomenal bodies with hearts endlessly pumping blood through them. He made our spirits alive so that we sense His presence and know that this is "Abba," Papa, Daddy, the Father who dearly loves us. We are His. As Paul puts it, "you are not your own . . . for you have been bought with a price" (1 Cor. 6:19-20).

We race for God. We live for God. In the scripture above, Paul says this is the attitude one should take hold of if one is "perfect." The Greek word doesn't carry the meaning of "flawless" but of "complete" or "mature." As we seek to love our Father with everything in us, we will slowly become more mature, more complete in our understanding of life from God's perspective. And each time we press on after a failure, our Father comes alongside us.

> The eyes of the Lord move to and fro throughout the earth that He may strongly support those whose heart is completely His. (2 Chron. 16:9)

2

> How blessed is the man who does not walk in the counsel of the wicked, nor stand in the path of sinners, nor sit in the seat of scoffers! But his delight is in the law of the Lord, and in His law he meditates day and night. He will be like a tree firmly planted by streams of water, which yields fruit in its season and its leaf does not wither; in whatever he does, he prospers. (Ps. 1:3)

A friend gave me a small potted plant, a species I'd never seen before. Its pink and green leaves were long and grass-like, and its trunk was thick and tough. A few months later I was surprised to see a different version of the same plant, six feet tall, in the hall of a building.

Goodness! If I repotted my plant to give the roots more space, and added rich soil, it would undoubtedly grow larger. Could it ever become as large as this one? I didn't know enough about plant biology to answer that. But taller, stronger, fuller? Certainly.

In the high-tech twenty-first century, the psalmist's picture of the tree drinking from the quiet stream can seem very unrelated to the way we conduct our lives. Yet this is how God has shown us that our lives are meant to be lived—meditating on His revelations of Himself and His ways in scripture; delighting in those revelations; growing strong as we push our roots deeply into this rich soil, and then yielding "fruit in its season." We love God by choosing a life of seeking Him and His strength, and by gradually becoming strong ourselves, useful servants with fruit to give to others.

3

> My son, give attention to my words; incline your ear to my sayings. Do not let them depart from your sight; keep them in the midst of your heart. (Prov. 4:20-21)

> Your servant meditates on Your statutes. Your testimonies also are my delight; they are my counselors. (Ps. 119:23-24)

Every thoughtful person realizes that our thoughts, opinions, attitudes, even our immediate reactions, are greatly impacted by what we have been reading, watching on TV, and seeing on the computer screen. And much that our eyes take in points us *away* from God's ways rather than towards them. Jesus taught, "The eye is the lamp of your body; when your eye is clear, your whole body is also full of light; but when it is bad, your body is also full of darkness" (Luke 11:34).

Yes, we need to read the Bible, to put the words of truth into our hearts. Our Father wants to speak with us daily, and often, and this is the most important way, the fullest way, in which He does it. The writer of the psalm above describes meditating on the scriptures, inclining his heart to them, treasuring them in his heart so that he won't sin against God. To do these acts of love for the Father, he must first read those scriptures.

How we get God's words into our hearts is between each one of us and our Father. *When* will we do it? Rising very early to create solid blocks of "quiet time" for prayer and Bible reading is a powerful, wonderful discipline practiced by many Christians. Yet others are discouraged when they don't succeed in following through with such a habit. During one period of my life, I met with God in a coffee shop for two or three afternoons a week with my Bible and a notebook. If we ask the Father, He will show each of us the best times and ways for reading and meditating on the scriptures.

4

> Do not fear, for I have redeemed you; I have called you by name; you are Mine! When you pass through the waters, I will be with you. When you walk through the fire, you will not be scorched, nor will the flame burn you . . . . [You] are precious in My sight . . . you are honored and I love you . . . everyone who is called by My name, and whom I have created for My glory . . . . (Is. 43:1-7)

God's words through Isaiah to the nation of Israel are to us as well. We too are precious and honored in God's sight. This is the love that we want to answer back with all our hearts.

The first, simplest, quickest way is with our thoughts and our words. This is prayer. When I'm alone with God, prayer isn't a signal to be over-concerned with how I'll position my body, or what I ought to include in my prayer, or how long my prayer should be. Prayer is, as much as possible, turning my thoughts from myself and looking to my wonderful God—rejoicing in His love, speaking love back, learning to wait and listen.

God loves our prayers! The clearest picture of the value of our prayers is what John records from his vision, twenty-four elders holding "golden bowls full of incense, which are the prayers of the saints" (Rev. 5:8). This helps our limited human minds to grasp that our prayers aren't just sounds dissipating into the air. In the spiritual realm, they are precious objects, caught and treasured by our Father, cherished as loving earthly parents might display and then preserve a child's crayon artwork done especially for them.

> May my prayer be counted as incense before You; the lifting of my hands as the evening offering. (Ps. 141:2)

5

> Then Moses went up with Aaron, Nadab, and Abihu, and seventy of the elders of Israel, and they saw the God of Israel; and under His feet there appeared to be a pavement of sapphire, as clear as the sky itself. Yet He did not stretch out His hand against the nobles of the sons of Israel; and they saw God, and they ate and drank. (Ex. 24:9-11)

> If anyone hears My voice and opens the door, I will come in to him, and will dine with him, and he with Me. (Rev. 3:20)

How in the world can human beings have a relationship with God, a spiritual being? A relationship in which the humans somehow experience the presence and the love and the thoughts of the God who created them? The fact remains that this is exactly the relationship God desires, and these sections from the scriptures help us understand the closeness He expects with us: the men saw God, and they ate and drank.

From living in Asia much of my life, I've learned that being a host in the Asian culture is a serious business. (I found out the hard way that even Taiwan university students expect more than a few bowls of snacks if they're invited to the house—there should have been real food, and plenty of it!) Jesus told a parable in which a man actually woke up his neighbor to procure food supplies for hosting an unexpected guest. And when Jesus Himself was the guest at the house of his good friend Lazarus, the friend's sister Martha made exhaustive preparations.

In Revelation 3:20, there are two hosts: us and Jesus. "I will come in to him and dine with him, and he with Me." We are the ones who prepare the best we have to offer, striving to have our hearts pure and our minds alert, ready to hear Him as we dine together. "And he with Me." Jesus is the host with infinitely more to offer. As David testifies in Psalm 36:8, "They drink their fill of the abundance of Your house."

We love God by accepting this picture of the relationship He wants to have with us, and opening the door. He will be the one to show us what this is going to mean.

6

> Trust in the Lord and do good; dwell in the land and cultivate faithfulness. Delight yourself in the Lord . . . . (Ps. 37:3-4)

> How blessed is the one whom You choose to bring near to You to dwell in Your courts. We will be satisfied with the goodness of Your house, Your holy temple. (Ps. 65:4)

The English language has a way to describe something (like a food, a beverage, or a style of art) which a person doesn't initially enjoy but grows to appreciate more and more with each encounter. We say that the thing is an acquired taste.

With no dishonor to the Lord, we could acknowledge that He Himself, or fellowship with Him, is an acquired taste. We read in the scriptures that David delighted in God (even danced for Him through the streets), and we've met Christians whose lives reflect a deep affection for God, and the scriptures tell us we *ought* to delight in the Lord. But perhaps we don't see this delight in ourselves. Not yet. Or not too often.

A taste for God, even a real hunger for Him, will grow as we seek to spend more private hours with Him. Some of those hours can be spent reading the Bible with Him: reading a section, then asking Him to help us understand it. And the Bible will show us an even higher model than godly Christians to fix our sights on—Father God delighting in *us*.

> I have loved you with an everlasting love; therefore I have drawn you with lovingkindness (Jer. 31:3).

> He will exult over you with joy, He will be quiet in His love, He will rejoice over you with shouts of joy (Zeph. 3:17).

> The Lord longs to be gracious to you . . . . How blessed are all those who long for Him (Is. 30:18).

> The prayer of the upright is His delight . . . . He loves one who pursues righteousness (Prov. 15:8-9).

7

> From the breath of God ice is made....Also with moisture He loads the thick cloud; He disperses the cloud of His lightning. And it changes direction, turning around by His guidance, that it may do whatever He commands it on the face of inhabited earth. (Job 37:10-12)

> You formed my inward parts; You wove me in my mother's womb. I will give thanks to You, for I am fearfully and wonderfully made; wonderful are Your works, and my soul knows it very well. (Ps. 139:13-14)

God is a spirit, invisible to human eyes. Yet as we press on to know God more deeply so that we can love Him more fully, the things our physical eyes do see will teach us much about His awesome power and wisdom. As one writer in scripture puts it, these physical wonders are just "the fringes of His ways," but it behooves us to look at them and press on to understand their complex nature. As we look, our souls can cry out, "Oh my God! You created this design!"

In today's world, however, sometimes we have to train ourselves to feel awe. For one thing, our textbooks, museums, and media are inundated with the lie that the wonders of the natural world are simply a pleasant result of the arbitrary forces of evolution. For another, scientific development has taken us so far in our understanding of the nature of the cell, that incredible powerhouse, and of the nature of the galaxies, that our minds get caught up in simply comprehending the mechanisms. Furthermore, technological advancement has made it possible for everyone to see photographs, on a daily basis, of life at the cellular level, of children in the womb, of objects in deep space—and the marvel we once felt has gradually faded.

But meditate on water. And think of the towering fir trees that dominate many western forests. Douglas firs may grow to be more than 400 feet high, which poses a huge problem of internal water transport, from roots to needle-thin leaves. But you see, water molecules are uniquely cohesive. They are polar, and adjacent molecules strongly attract each other. Also, hydrogen bonds form between them, so that a column of water has the tensile strength of a metal wire.

May all love and honor be given to the Creator of water, a substance that defeats the tremendous forces of gravity to travel up trees and cornstalks and grapevines and flowers and bring life to all the earth!

8

> So let us know, let us press on to know the Lord. His going forth is as certain as the dawn; and He will come to us like the rain, like the spring rain watering the earth. (Hos. 6:3)

The prophet Hosea exhorts God's people to press on to know God more. And this knowledge is clearly a process, a journey accomplished over time. It isn't a search *for* God—we Christians have been born of God's Spirit, and He is our Father, as Jesus said. But knowing God deeply will happen during the hours and days and years of prayer, the miles of walking in obedience to what He teaches us in those times of prayer. The scriptures will reveal an abundance of truth to us *about* the God we seek to know. Nonetheless, we will only delight His heart by pressing on to know Him as counselor and friend.

We Christians have spirits sensitive to the Holy Spirit, who lives in us—and we have bodies with muscles that cramp up, minds that get restless when we venture into times of prayer. God's loyalty to us is absolute, but ours is sometimes very fleeting. The same was true of the Israelites God was addressing through the prophet Hosea: "What shall I do with you, O Judah? For your loyalty is like a morning cloud, and like the dew which goes away early" (Hos. 6:4).

God's loyalty, on the other hand, is compared to the absolutes of the earth's rotation and its revolution. The night may seem endless for the child waiting for Christmas morning, for the anxious insomniac—but dawn *will* come. In the long winter, it is hard to believe that spring will ever arrive. Yet it does.

So let us wait in patience, and agree with David's prayer in Psalm 27:

> Hear, O Lord, when I cry with my voice, and be gracious to me and answer me. When You said, "Seek My face," my heart said to You, "Your face, O Lord, I shall seek." (Ps. 27:7-8)

9

> Enter His gates with thanksgiving and His courts with praise. Give thanks to Him, bless His name. For the Lord is good, His lovingkindness is everlasting and His faithfulness to all generations. (Ps. 100:4-5)

> I will give thanks to You, O Lord my God, with all my heart, and will glorify Your name forever. For Your lovingkindness toward me is great, and You have delivered my soul from the depths of Sheol. (Ps. 86:12-13)

If we opened the door to find a much-loved, specially awaited friend or relative, there would be mutual shouts of delight and strong embraces. The task we were doing, the TV show or book we were enjoying, would be easily tossed aside for the welcome new activity of welcoming this dear one. In contrast, moving into a time of prayer is not always accomplished with such enthusiasm and smoothness. We don't simply open a physical door and find a smiling friend waiting to hug us. Our Friend is there. But to get from the earthly plane (with its claims on our time and attention) to a plane where we have undivided fellowship with the Spirit of God, we humans usually need a kind of "decompression chamber."

The "chamber" is a time of thanksgiving and praise. "Enter His gates with thanksgiving and His courts with praise." *Who* is this wonderful God that the eyes of my heart were created to see? He's the God whose mercy is from everlasting to everlasting. He's a God of faithfulness, of justice. He's a God of tender love, of forgiveness, of amazing patience toward all He has made. He's my Provider.

We speak aloud these praises of God's character; we express our wonder at how these attributes proved true in God's ways with His people in the Bible. And we thank Him for particular instances in our own lives where we have known His faithfulness, His love, His provision, and so on.

These praises are our embraces. And they do become mutual. As our spirits intentionally reach out for God, God floods us with a deeper knowledge of Himself, and of these aspects of who He is.

Have you entered the "praise chamber" yet today?

10

> Now, Israel, what does the Lord your God require from you, but to fear the Lord your God, to walk in all His ways and love Him, and to serve the Lord your God with all your heart and with all your soul, and to keep the Lord's commandments and His statutes which I am commanding you today for your good? (Deut. 10:12-13)

Throughout the accounts of God's dealings with the Israelites that He led out of Egypt, the people were taught that loving God and walking in His ways went together. Moses pleaded with them to obey God's laws and statutes and warned of the terrible consequences of ignoring them.

What attitude does God want us to have towards the words He has given us? In Psalm 119, the writer says, "O how I love Your law! It is my meditation all the day" (v. 197). For most of us, that claim would be extravagant, and we wouldn't make it. And yet we remember times when certain words of scripture really touched us, or pointed us in the right direction. And we *want* to love the Bible more.

Psalm 119, the Bible's longest song, is a huge catalog of the psalmist's responses of love for God's words. Sometimes the psalmist seems to be speaking of new words, fresh directions. "I rise before dawn and cry for help; I wait for your words" (v. 147). But usually he is referring to the Law and the Prophets. "Seven times a day I praise You, because of Your righteous ordinances. Those who love Your law have great peace, and nothing causes them to stumble" (vv. 164-165).

One response of the psalmist to God's words is gratitude. "I shall give thanks to You with uprightness of heart, when I learn Your righteous judgments" (v. 7). Later on, he gets more enthusiastic in describing his appreciation. "The law of Your mouth is better to me than thousands of gold and silver pieces" (v. 72). "I love your commandments above gold, yes, above fine gold. Therefore I esteem right all Your precepts concerning everything, I hate every false way" (vv. 127-128).

The psalmist had a smaller set of scriptures to be thankful for; we have the Old and New Testaments. In China today, some house churches still lack even one Bible, and a young evangelist sometimes memorizes a single book of it and travels from church to church, speaking it out. If you're reading this devotional, you probably have a Bible of your own next to you on the table. Have you learned yet how precious its words are?

Love the Lord by asking Him to help you develop a deeper appreciation for the pages of that book on the table.

> Open my eyes, that I may behold wonderful things from Your law. (Ps. 119:18)

11

Praise the Lord! Praise the Lord, O my soul! I will praise the Lord while I live; I will sing praises to my God while I have my being. (Ps. 146:1-2)

Then I looked, and I heard the voice of many angels around the throne and the living creatures and the elders; and the number of them was myriads of myriads, and thousands and thousands, saying with a loud voice, "Worthy is the Lamb that was slain to receive power and riches and wisdom and might and honor and glory and blessing." (Rev. 5:11-12)

We love God by continually presenting Him with the offering of the angels and the others in John's vision. Jesus, the Lamb of God, is worthy to receive such things from us, from me.

He is worthy to receive "power" and "might" from me—all of my energies, and perseverance, and endurance.

He is worthy to receive my "riches"—control of all my financial assets.

He is worthy to receive my "wisdom"—the use of all the creativity and talents that I have now, and the gifts in me yet to be developed.

He is worthy of all honor—in every daily decision, my absolute obedience to God my King.

He is worthy to receive glory from me for the works accomplished by His mighty power in me, and in all creation.

He is worthy to receive my blessing and praise. I will sing to Him, shout to Him, dance to Him, play an instrument to Him!

12

> We love, because He first loved us. If someone says, "I love God," and hates his brother, he is a liar; for the one who does not love his brother whom he has seen, cannot love God whom he has not seen. And this commandment we have from Him, that the one who loves God should love his brother also. Whoever believes that Jesus is the Christ is born of God, and whoever loves the Father loves the child born of Him. (1 John 4:19-5:1)

When we read these words of scripture with open hearts, they often hit us like a ton of bricks. We know we stand accused. That person who wronged us many years ago; the relative we try hard to avoid; the colleague or neighbor who gets us so angry—the word "hate" makes us wince, but the Lord of hearts knows the truth about our feelings for these people.

Satan would have us wallow in self-condemnation, or shrug off the impossibility of loving these unlovable ones. But our hearts cry out that we're not liars, that we do love God. And so we do, to a limited extent. Yet the Holy Spirit would draw us further on in honoring both of the great commandments: loving God with all our heart, soul, mind, and strength, and loving our neighbors as ourselves.

The book of James teaches us that scripture can be a mirror for our "natural face," so that we can see "what kind of a person" we are and take action (James 1:23-25). John's letter above reminds us of what is commanded in God's kingdom: "the one who loves God should love his brother also." John also tells us that this is a reality in God's kingdom: "Whoever loves the Father loves the child born of Him." When we let this scripture be our mirror, it will expose our love debts toward others. We honor God by believing His word and confessing that love *can* be and *must* be released in us toward all those who are loved by the Father.

13

> When my heart was embittered and I was pierced within, then I was senseless and ignorant; I was like a beast before You. (Ps. 73:21-22)

As we seek to love God with all our heart, we learn to recognize some forms of spiritual heart disease. A major one is bitterness.

Bitterness usually has its roots in a sense of injustice. Righteous Job admits his own bitterness about the undeserved calamities that have struck him and his family (Job 10:1-3). In the psalm above, David explains that he had felt envy toward arrogant and wicked men who were living in prosperity. Bitterness is often directed toward individuals who we feel have received more benefits than we have, It thrives in families, as with Cain and Abel, Jacob and Esau, Rachel and Leah. And it may be directed toward someone who withheld love or honor, and perhaps gave us the opposite instead.

Few of us lack our own examples of personal injustice, and often there are people we've never quite forgiven for what they did or did not do. This creates a spiritual heart disease which makes us "senseless and ignorant," "like a beast" in God's presence. God speaks and we don't perceive it, or we don't understand Him.

As the psalm above continues, David tells God, "Nevertheless I am continually with You; You have taken hold of my right hand. With Your counsel You will guide me, and afterward receive me into glory" (vv. 23-24). One day many years ago I was jumping up and down on my small trampoline when the Spirit of God suddenly showed me something: a grudge I'd harbored against an old friend for almost a decade. God's question to me was whether I would like to have this grudge removed, as He was ready to do so. My response was an ecstatic "Yes!" Seconds later, I leaped off the trampoline and ran upstairs to look up an old phone number and immediately extend love and forgiveness across the Pacific Ocean.

Let God uproot all bitterness in your heart.

> The troubles of my heart are enlarged; bring me out of my distresses. Look upon my affliction and my trouble, and forgive all my sins. (Ps. 25:17-18)

14

> Why do you call Me, "Lord, Lord," and do not do what I say? Everyone who comes to Me and hears My words and acts on them, I will show you whom he is like: he is like a man building a house, who dug deep and laid a foundation on the rock; and when a flood occurred, the torrent burst against that house and could not shake it, because it had been well built. (Luke 6:46-48)

Those who seek to love God with all that is within them learn quickly that love cannot be separated from obedience. It isn't a case of summoning up a warm feeling to assure God—and ourselves—that we really do love Him. Rather, it's accepting the yoke of obedience, of servanthood. "I'm yours, Lord. What's on Your agenda? What are we doing today? What are we doing right now?"

The gospel of Luke records Jesus' parable of the four seeds. Jesus explains that the seed is the word of God, and that "the seed in the good soil, these are the ones who have heard the word in an honest and good heart, and hold it fast, and bear fruit with perseverance . . . . So take care how you listen; for whoever has, to him more shall be given . . ." (Luke 8:15, 18).

When we recognize that God is telling us to do something and we say, "Yes, Lord," and do it, we are loving Him. We are living like the man who dug deep in order to build his house on a rock. Continued obedience digs deep. As we obey, we'll find ourselves shoveling aside the things that get in the way—the selfish attitudes, the demanding preferences, the fears and uncertainties, the hidden sins. When we stop digging for a time, some sand blows back; disobedience has consequences, always. But by God's grace we can repent and set ourselves once again at loving God and obeying Him.

Continued obedience will build us into stronger, better servants for our Master, ready to love and serve Him in more ways that He will show us.

> If you keep My commandments, you will abide in My love; just as I have kept My Father's commandments and abide in His love. (John 15:10)

15

> Who may ascend the hill of the Lord? And who may stand in His holy place? He who has clean hands and a pure heart, who has not lifted up his soul to falsehood and has not sworn deceitfully. (Ps. 24:3-4)
>
> Blessed are the pure in heart, for they shall see God. (Matt. 5:8)

In the section of scripture known as "the beatitudes" (Matt. 5:3-11), Jesus calls several groups of people "blessed," or "happy"—the poor in spirit, those who mourn, the gentle or humble, and so on. Sometimes we're not sure what His words mean, but one phrase is crystal clear: the pure in heart. When I used to read Jesus' teaching above, the "pure in heart" was a group with which I felt no identification at all. I had mourned, I had sometimes been humble and merciful, and I had had spurts of hungering for righteousness. But I felt that the pure in heart must be a very special group which could never include me.

Yet a pure heart is precisely what we are called to have. The one who has "clean hands and a pure heart" is the one who can "ascend the hill of the Lord." Jesus calls us to a radical purity, one that the world will scorn. To keep free from the sin of sexual lust, I may need to turn my head from a scene before me, or close my eyes during a film, or leave a party. To keep free from the sin of greed or coveting, I may need to keep close watch on my thoughts as I browse through shopping malls, magazines, catalogs, investment information. To keep free from murdering someone in my heart, I will be continually rejecting angry attitudes, choosing forgiveness instead, and refusing to join others in their hate and accusation.

Purity of heart isn't a resting place after a long marathon. It's like the peak of Mount Everest, where Edmund Hillary posed for a photograph gripping his country's flag; the photo shows him standing hunched forward, eyes closed, because of the powerful winds beating against him. The Evil One will never give us a break, will never let up. But when our hearts are pure, we will stand, and we will see God.

16

> Both riches and honor come from You, and You rule over all, and in Your hand is power and might; and it lies in Your hand to make great, and to strengthen everyone. (1 Chr. 29:12)

Love the Lord with all my strength? Sometimes we feel anything but strong. At those times, perhaps we lean on a bit of theology gleaned from the classic Sunday school song "Jesus Loves Me": "Little ones to Him belong; they are weak, but He is strong." That's right, we remind ourselves, Jesus is the strong one; we're supposed to be weak.

Fasten your seatbelts. This theology is flawed.

As a created being, one also born again as a child of God, I possess an amazing physical body designed to last a number of decades, and a spirit that will live forever. My body thrives on oxygen, food, and water; my spirit thrives on intimacy with God. When I don't consume the physical and spiritual nourishment that I need, I'm indeed weak. But this weakness is an unhealthy state! Healthy bodies are strong, not weak; good habits keep them that way. Healthy Christians are strong, not weak. They live lives in which quality times with God are top priority, not permitted to be squeezed out.

Certainly, when I'm strong, it's *God's* strength in me. There's never a question of doing something in "my" strength versus "His" strength. It's *all* His strength. I didn't manufacture any strength, or create the process, or produce the raw materials. My body, my spirit, my strength are all gifts from God. And I am their steward.

"Love the Lord . . . with all your strength." God's strength in me is now my strength. And God tells me to offer it back to Him, for the sake of His kingdom. Not a tithe of it—*all* of it.

17

> With all my heart I have sought You; do not let me wander from Your commandments. Your word have I treasured in my heart, that I may not sin against You. (Ps. 119:10-11)
>
> I have restrained my feet from every evil way, that I may keep Your word. I have not turned aside from Your ordinances, for You have taught me. (Ps. 119:101-102)
>
> Establish my footsteps in Your word, and do not let any iniquity have dominion over me. (Ps. 119:133)

Some Christians have developed an opinion that the only value of God's law was to set up an impossible standard so that we would see how much we needed grace. These folks secretly doubt their ability to obey God's commands, so they avoid thinking about them. Instead, they focus all their attention on the saving and redeeming work of Christ.

The psalmist had no such prejudice toward the law, no fear of looking at the teachings of the scriptures and finding that he fell short. Even before Christ came, the early Jews already understood the concept of grace, of provision being made so that their sins could be forgiven. This was one of the major themes running through the ritual sacrifices and holy days that God had decreed through Moses. The scriptures told of how time after time God's people had sinned, as a group and individually—even King David had committed adultery and murder—and God had forgiven.

The writer of the psalm above read the scriptures because he loved God and wanted to know exactly how to obey Him. He knew that the commandments were not impossible to keep, even though he would sometimes fail in keeping them. And he knew that to choose obedience was to choose life.

> For this commandment which I command you today is not too difficult for you, nor is it out of reach . . . . But the word is very near you, in your mouth and in your heart, that you may observe it. (Deut. 30:11, 14)

18

> When the living creatures give glory and honor and thanks to Him who sits on the throne, to Him who lives forever and ever, the twenty-four elders will fall down before Him who sits on the throne, and will worship Him who lives forever and ever, and will cast their crowns before the throne, saying, "Worthy are You, our Lord and our God, to receive glory and honor and power; for You created all things, and because of Your will they existed, and were created. (Rev. 4:9-11)

The elders in John's vision declare that the Lord is worthy to receive "glory and honor and power." Many of our modern songs of worship have phrases like "Glory to our God," "we glorify You," "You are worthy of all honor," "we honor You." Not too many speak of lifting up power, or offering power, to God. After all, the scriptures teach that "power belongs to God" (Ps. 62:11). Yet they also teach that He gives power to the humans He created. "The God of Israel Himself gives strength and power to the people. Blessed be God!" (Ps. 68:35). Jesus tells his disciples, "I give you power to tread upon serpents and scorpions, and over all the power of the enemy," and later, "You shall receive power when the Holy Spirit has come upon you" (Luke 10:19, Acts 1:8).

According to Cruden's Complete Concordance, the word "power" in the Bible can refer either to "rule or authority" or "might and strength."[2] As we saw in the twentieth century, when powerful armies invade countries unable to resist them, the two meanings become synonymous. Our God has authority because of His mighty strength. And He gives Christians both authority and strength to do the "good works which God prepared beforehand so that we would walk in them" (Eph. 2:10).

We love and honor God when we acknowledge that all our strength comes from Him and then *live it back to Him*. As the scripture from Revelation above tells us, God is worthy to receive all the power that is in us, because He created us. We are His, created to do the good works He has prepared, created for His glory.

19

> All of your works shall give thanks to You, O Lord, and all
> Your godly ones shall bless You. (Ps. 145:10)

Most people admit to having a special appreciation in their hearts for either the sea or the mountains, and sometimes both. We are awed by the vastness of the sea, its continual movement in response to the moon's pull, the knowledge that its depths are teeming with life; we gaze at the towering mountains, visible for miles around, created by cataclysmic events under the earth, glorious against the horizon. Because even the memory of these wonders can lift us from our daily concerns, some of us who live near neither oceans nor mountains hang photographic calendars or landscape paintings on our walls that we can rest our eyes on.

We do well to let these wonders cause us to lift up our eyes and our hearts to the God who created them.

> By awesome deeds You answer us in righteousness, O God of our salvation, You who are the trust of all the ends of the earth and of the farthest sea; Who establishes the mountains by His strength, being girded with might; Who stills the roaring of the seas, the roaring of their waves, and the tumult of the peoples. They who dwell in the ends of the earth stand in awe of Your signs; You make the dawn and the sunset shout for joy. (Ps. 65: 5-8)

Love God by joining the dawn and the sunset and all of creation in their praise of Him!

20

In my own experience, God's ways can be so unimaginable as to be called bizarre. At age 58, I was trying to muster faith and quell my anxiety over the upcoming termination of an 18-year teaching position when God designed a remarkable series of events. It began with my decision to encourage a fellow teacher by attending an exhibit of his art at a small gallery. (I'd never visited a private gallery in my life.) There, I fell in love with (and subsequently bought) a painting by another artist, the one who leased the gallery; I was told I'd got in just ahead of another interested buyer. This visit led to my attending other shows at the gallery, where I eventually met the man who had missed purchasing my painting. Gary turned out to be a former colleague I hadn't seen in a decade. He now had his own language school and was eager to offer me a job there.

> "For My thoughts are not your thoughts, nor are your ways
> My ways," declares the Lord. "For as the heavens are higher
> than the earth, so are My ways higher than your ways and
> My thoughts than your thoughts. (Isa. 55:8-9)

Can you recall times when even a tragic event brought far-reaching blessings no one could have imagined? And even then we only see in part.

Acknowledging the limitations of our understanding clears away the mental traffic jams in our prayer times, times when we want to focus on hearing God's words for today but our minds are stuck in worries about unresolved problems in our lives or the lives of others.

Love God by acknowledging to yourself and to Him that in every event of life you only see the tiniest part of a huge picture. Affirm to Him that His ways are higher and that you trust Him.

21

> "Come now, and let us reason together," says the Lord. "Though your sins are as scarlet, they will be as white as snow." (Is. 1:18)

> If we confess our sins, He is faithful and righteous to forgive us our sins and to cleanse us from all unrighteousness. (1 John 1:9)

The most amazing piece of good news in the Bible is that Jesus died for my sins, took the punishment for them so that I could be eternally reconciled with God.

Another piece of news, truly awesome if I consider it, is that Jesus wants to continually wash me of the filthy sins I do. I can't sit at the table with Him and His Father with dirty feet, and only He can make me clean. I need to submit to letting Jesus see my filthy sins and wash me clean enough for fellowship with Him.

The disciple Peter objected to the original foot washing, saying, "'Never shall you wash my feet.' Jesus answered him, 'If I do not wash you, you have no part with Me.' Simon Peter said to Him, 'Lord, then wash not only my feet, but also my hands and my head.' Jesus said to him, 'He who has bathed needs only to wash his feet, but is completely clean'" (John 13:8-10).

I'm a disciple, and Jesus doesn't expect me to go on a muddy roll. He looks for my loyalty and obedience, and my goal is to give Him those things with all that is within me. Yet I will still, and often, have sins to confess. Maybe I've acted exactly as He told me not to; or I've failed to do as He commanded; or I've spoken words that poured evil into the air. Or maybe I'm embarrassed even to come to the table because I'm still musing on sinful thoughts that have entered my mind, thoughts I should have rejected minutes or hours or days ago.

As faithful servants who don't want to miss a word that the Master would say to us, we do well to echo David's prayer on a regular basis:

> Search me, O God, and know my heart: try me and know my thoughts: and see if there be any wicked way in me, and lead me in the way everlasting. (Ps. 139:23-24 KJV)

22

> I delight in loyalty rather than sacrifice, in the knowledge of God rather than burnt offerings. (Hos. 6:6)

> The prayer of the upright is His delight. (Prov. 15:8)

These scriptures reveal an amazing truth: God delights in our efforts to reach toward Him, to try to know Him more deeply. He has always delighted in this. He directed Moses to institute a number of regular offerings which taught the Israelites to understand and practice thanksgiving and confession of sin. But God often warned His people that they had missed the primary point by focusing on the secondaries. They had carefully measured out their tithes, had shown up at the appropriate times with offerings of grains, pigeons, or domestic animals—and considered they had done what God required of them. Yet they hadn't stretched their minds toward God to learn His heart, to know what would please Him, to truly become a light to the nations around them.

For Christians today, there aren't complex sacrificial rituals to distract our focus. Instead, there are programs: wonderful church services, Bible studies, home groups, and conferences. These sometimes excellent programs are composed of chopped-up segments of time: song / Bible verse / prayer / song / sermon / sharing / announcements / chatting—and so on. A lot is said *about* our God, yet in a given hour, there are often only a few minutes of silence when God's people sit in His presence, give Him their undivided attention, and press closer to hear Him speak to their hearts.

Love the Lord by majoring in time spent with Him alone, in prayer and meditation, and by minoring in excellent programs. To paraphrase a popular writer, the main thing to remember is to keep the main thing the main thing.[3]

23

> As for you, my son Solomon, know the God of your father, and serve Him with a whole heart and a willing mind; for the Lord searches all hearts, and understands every intent of the thoughts. (1 Chr. 28:9)

For those who don't yet understand the deep love of the Father, the idea of a God who knows every intent of their thoughts may be embarrassing and even frightening. People who have allowed certain sins to set up housekeeping may feel resentment that God would want these things confessed and cut out of their lives. Starting with that resentment and spurred on by a determination not to face God's disapproval, they build mental barriers and plaster them over with the justifications they hope will keep out God's truth. ("Everyone cheats this way nowadays." "It's not actually a physical relationship." "It's too much to expect. I will never, never forgive him.")

Many of us now shudder at memories of how effective these self-imposed prisons have been at different times in our lives. While providing no defense whatever from the eyes of God, these rebellious attitudes kept us living in a dim half-light, perhaps even as we carried out regular religious activities. Meanwhile the sins became like cancerous growths, secretly spreading into other areas of our lives.

As we seek to love God more, we willingly fling open all the hidden recesses of our minds. We don't ever want to start furnishing new prisons cells. We welcome the searching light of the Lord and want to rid ourselves of every sin which that light reveals. This obedience has a rich reward.

> If we say that we have fellowship with Him, and yet walk in darkness, we lie and do not practice the truth; but if we walk in the light, as He Himself is in the Light, we have fellowship with one another, and the blood of Jesus His Son cleanses us from all sin. (1 John 1:6-7)

24

> My son, if you receive my words, and treasure my commandments within you, make your ear attentive to wisdom, incline your heart to understanding; for if you cry for discernment, lift your voice for understanding; if you seek her as silver, and search for her as for hidden treasures; then you will discern the fear of the Lord, and discover the knowledge of God. (Prov. 2:1-5)

The modern-day equivalent of the acquisition of silver and hidden treasure is no less exacting and time-consuming than it was in King Solomon's day. Financial security for oneself and one's family remains a basic goal which is deemed worthy of considerable effort. Breadwinners may work long hours, even welcoming overtime hours for the extra pay. Successful investors in the stock market expect to invest hours of time in learning about each company's financial position.

We can only grow in our love for God as we grow in our experiential knowledge of Him. And scripture tells us to expect that the process will be as demanding as our modern "search for silver." The verses above include active verbs that describe the effort it will require to take charge of our natural human inclinations and get them centered on God.

"**Incline** your ear to wisdom." Deliberately turn *toward* the Holy Spirit's whispers, and away from the TV show you were watching.

"**Apply** your heart to understanding." This won't come easy. Application to learning a challenging new job takes determined concentration; performing that job well may take discipline in shrugging off boredom to stay focused sometimes. Furthermore, the natural mind does not readily submit to spiritual discipline; yet the goal is far greater than a paycheck, than financial security.

"**Cry** for discernment," "lift up your voice (or "shout aloud") for understanding." You'll need to do this. The physical pleasures and cultural pastimes around you—tasty snacks, movies, Internet games, novels, and more—will forever be crying out for your easy, pleasant participation. Your own cries to God had best be spoken aloud, so that they'll be loud enough to block out these other voices.

Turn your ear, apply your heart, cry out! God hears and He will answer.

> Blessed are those who hunger and thirst after righteousness, for they shall be satisfied. (Matt. 5:6)

25

> I opened my mouth wide and panted, for I longed for Your commandments. (Ps. 119:131)

> I rejoice at Your word as one who finds great spoil. (Ps. 119:162)

The enthusiasm and delight of the psalmist for the scriptures makes us smile, possibly in amazement. Could anyone be this excited about reading the Bible? Yet we may recall moments when we felt like that about something God showed us in a passage of scripture.

When I open my mouth wide, it's generally to put food into it. Could our hearts learn to be as eager for God's words as our stomachs are for our next meal? Many Christians have learned that yes, they can. Sometimes a period of fasting can be a training ground, a time when the pray-er asks God to teach his or her heart to ache with a hunger for God the way the body is currently aching for food. When hunger for God becomes a part of our daily lives, when we crave time with God and His word the way we crave coffee or chocolate or some other beloved "staple" of life, we too will be mentally opening our mouths and panting. And when our hearts are properly hungry for the words of truth, we'll agree with the psalmist—"How sweet are Your words to my taste! Yes, sweeter than honey to my mouth!" (Ps.119:103).

Sometimes I can get enthusiastic about a theme in scripture and chase it all over the Bible. I might use a word concordance (looking to see other passages where "rejoice" occurs, for instance), or I might enjoy just flipping back to where I think I remember having read it. When I first began contemplating God's great commandment to love Him with my heart, soul, mind, and strength, I bought a brand new Bible and began color-coding every verse that seemed to be related to the subject. I have the sort of mind that enjoys finding patterns, and whenever I sighted a new, related truth, I would indeed "rejoice . . . as one who finds great spoil."

Love the Lord by asking Him to cultivate your delight in His written words. And let Him do His work in you and in your life as He answers that prayer.

26

> I will give them one heart, and put a new spirit within them. And I will take the heart of stone out of their flesh and give them a heart of flesh, that they may walk in my statutes and keep My ordinances and do them. Then they will be My people, and I shall be their God. (Ezek. 11:19-20)

"A heart of stone" is a figurative phrase but one that could probably be understood in any language. Each of us knows how a stone heart exercises itself in our own lives, and what we do to make that heart harder, and colder.

We build hard attitudes toward those who might want something from us. We leap to set up solid defenses against those who might hurt us or threaten our position. We make cold judgments about people in advance, before they've opened their mouths, so that our love isn't available to them. And when we do these things to "the least of these," it's always a reflection of our heart toward God. It demonstrates that we've made idols of our own attitudes and judgments.

According to the scripture above, God is in the business of heart transplants. He wants to give us hearts that are soft toward Him and others, hearts that—like His own—can be bruised, hurt, broken again and again. We may resist the exchange. And in fact, it cannot take place without our full cooperation.

Ezekiel's prophetic message goes on to say, "Repent and turn away from all your transgressions, so that iniquity may not become a stumbling block to you. Cast away from you all your transgressions which you have committed and make yourselves a new heart and new spirit! For why will you die, O house of Israel?" (Ezek. 18: 30-31).

So both we and our Maker are the makers of our new heart. And as with a physical transplant recipient, we need to have the old heart removed before receiving the new one.

It's one more way in which we lose our life for Christ's sake in order to find it.

27

> [Elijah] . . . went . . . forty days and forty nights unto Horeb the mount of God . . . . And behold, the Lord passed by, and a great and strong wind rent the mountains, and brake in pieces the rocks before the Lord; but the Lord was not in the wind: and after the wind an earthquake; but the Lord was not in the earthquake: And after the earthquake a fire; but the Lord was not in the fire: and after the fire a still small voice. And it was so, when Elijah heard it that he wrapped his face in his mantle, and went out, and stood in the entering in of the cave. And, behold, there came a voice unto him, and said, What doest thou here, Elijah? (1 Kin. 19:8-13 KJV)

When the prophet Elijah ran for his life from the death threats of Queen Jezebel, he collapsed after a few days in suicidal exhaustion. But after an angel arrived to feed and strengthen him, he continued his journey. His destination was Horeb, the "mountain of God," the site where God had so often met Moses, beginning with the burning bush. When Elijah arrived, he knew what to listen for, because he knew God's voice. The explosive atmospheric events preceding it may have terrified him, but they did not confuse him. He waited for the voice he had come to hear.

Unlike Elijah, I have sometimes been confused. As a teenage Christian, for example, I found it impossible to separate a charged atmosphere from the presence of God. Swelling organ music in services and round-the-campfire times at church retreats would get my emotions soaring. It may be that this rush of feeling was triggered by God, but I never searched further, listened closely for what He might say. Instead, I simply embraced the sweet, warm sensations which only came in these specially prepared settings. The rest of my life showed no evidence of being changed and directed by God's love.

In seeking to love God more, it is good to make time to be with others to worship and pray. These can be some of our "date times" with God. But we should resist the trap of simply attending meetings as spectators, hoping that a bit of holy atmosphere will raise our spirits. When our spirits are thirsty, it's time to drink at the well of Christ. The emotional thrill of hearing beautiful music, the intellectual satisfaction of hearing an eloquent sermon, the fun of hearing (or reading) moving accounts of other Christians' adventures with God are all weak substitutes. In some churches, perhaps it's time to turn the sound systems way, way down so that people can remember to listen for God's still small voice.

28

> I confess my iniquity; I am full of anxiety because of my sin. (Ps. 38:18)

When our bodies feel hot and "feverish," we take our temperatures and may discover that yes, indeed, we do have a fever. This elevated body temperature may indicate bad news—possibly a viral or bacterial infection. But the fever itself, the elevated temperature, is a blessing in that it tells us something in us may be amiss. Thus we can take steps accordingly.

Anxiety is a fever of the soul. In Psalm 38, David is weighed down with the realizations of his sins. "I am benumbed and badly crushed; I groan because of the agitation of my heart" (v. 8).

In my own life, I struggle against wrong attitudes toward others: frustration when they don't seem to value or admire me, anger when I see their wrong actions, fear that they will lash out at me or—worse—discount me. When I don't acknowledge these attitudes quickly, and accept God's pardon, they get shoved into dark corners of my mind and fester.

In learning to walk more closely with the Lord, I've come to recognize anxiety the way a mother notices her child's hot and sweaty face. It's a symptom, a signal. The mother reaches for the thermometer. I'm learning to reach toward my Lord. "Lord, what is this anxiety about? What, or whom, am I afraid of, or angry about? A recent event? A future confrontation?"

We love the Lord by keeping our souls swept clean, confessing the sins He shows us, so that our communication with Him remains clear and unbroken.

> If I should say, "My foot has slipped," Your lovingkindness, O Lord, will hold me up. When my anxious thoughts multiply within me, Your consolations delight my soul. (Ps. 94:18-19)

29

> Sing to Him, sing praises to Him; speak of all His wonders. Glory in His holy name; let the heart of those who seek the Lord be glad. Seek the Lord and His strength; seek His face continually. Remember His wonderful deeds which He has done, His marvels and the judgments of His mouth. (1 Chr. 16:9-12)

Christians have begun to recognize that they tend to express much more heart-felt enthusiasm at a sports event than they do in a worship service. Yet when a well-meaning song leader urges them to "sing it again, with feeling!" they are right to wince. We don't want to manufacture a showy performance for God.

The Lord looks at our hearts, at what is underneath our public display of musical worship or expressions of prayer. And only a desire to love and honor Him with all our hearts will be an acceptable offering of praise.

Nevertheless, the scripture above reminds us that it is right to get excited and emotional, to "be glad" as we "seek His face." Sometimes church services aid us in our seeking, and sometimes they unintentionally distract us from it; but in our private times with God, we can pull out all the stops.

Verses 9 and 10 above can also be rendered "Meditate on all His wonders. Boast in His holy name." Love God by often speaking to Him in prayer about all the wonderful things He has done in Your life and the lives of others. "Seek His face continually"—thank Him quietly out loud as you walk away from a situation where you have seen Him work.

Seek Him continually, and be glad. What a privilege! What a Lord!

> Splendor and majesty are before Him, strength and joy are in His place. (1 Chr. 16:27)

30

> But you, beloved, building yourselves up on your most holy faith, praying in the Holy Spirit, keep yourselves in the love of God . . . . (Jude 20-21)

> Be anxious for nothing, but in everything by prayer and supplication with thanksgiving let your requests be made known to God. (Phil. 4:6)

Our experience of what prayer is, or can be, depends a great deal on the churches we have been part of. Not what the churches *taught* about prayer, but how, and how much, they actually engaged in it when people met together. How often I meet Christians who say they couldn't possibly pray aloud in a group, either because they have no idea how to proceed, or because they are afraid their words won't be elegant enough to please God or others.

I attended one church in Taipei for several years, and I've always credited those Christians with teaching me how to pray. Wednesday evening prayer meetings were well attended, and the entire ninety minutes was given over to prayer: prayer by the person up front; prayer by each of us speaking our own prayers aloud simultaneously; prayer in small groups huddled together in the pews; prayers as we sang songs of worship—"This time, let's have the women sing and the men pray." Included were times of silence so that our spirits could listen to God.

And that was just the regular mid-week prayer meeting. There were more prayer times. Not only did every gathering in the church include times of prayer, but usually the gathering was preceded by a 15-20 minute meeting *to pray for* that gathering time!

These folks knew how to pray. We need to know, too, from ongoing, abundant practice. Jude writes that prayer is part of how we keep ourselves in the love of God. Prayer keeps us on the channel where our spirits are aware of His incredible love, and we ourselves can speak, think, and live back to Him all love and adoration.

31

> He gives strength to the weary, and to him who lacks might He increases power. Though youths grow weary and tired, and vigorous young men stumble badly, yet those who wait for the Lord will gain new strength; they will mount up with wings like eagles, they will run and not get tired, they will walk and not become weary. (Is. 40:29-31)

I'm a child of God, and I have a present and future inheritance of everything I need for life and godliness (2 Pet. 1:3). My inheritance includes access to a continual renewal of strength, strength for the present task and for the long haul.

Without God's strength in me, I'd be weak. More than that, I'd be dead. Every cell in my body contains a powerhouse of energy, created and sustained by the unfathomable God who loves me. With God's mighty power in me, I breathe, digest food, run, dance, fight battles, and persevere in bleak circumstances. However, my body and spirit were not designed to be self-sufficient. The body requires a regular intake of food and water, plus regular sleep and exercise to rest and renew the mechanisms. The spirit requires a continual renewal of spiritual strength, and it's only obtained by waiting on God.

If we refused to eat, we would weaken and die. This applies to everyone. If we neglect our basic need of solid time spent alone in His presence, we *will* be spiritually weak. (Again, there are no exceptions. This is how things work in God's world.) We will grow tired and weary. Our "ministries" will have nothing of God's life in them. Eventually we will stumble badly. Our storage tank of strength will run dry, and only because we neglected our first duty as servants of God: waiting on God.

> Wait for the Lord; be strong, and let your heart take courage; yes, wait for the Lord. (Ps. 27:14)

32

> Jesus came to the disciples and found them sleeping, and said to Peter, "So you men could not keep watch with Me for one hour? Keep watching and praying, that you may not enter into temptation; the spirit is willing, but the flesh is weak." (Matt. 26:40)

Jesus hoped that His closest friends on earth would be able to support Him in prayer for a few hours in His most difficult time of struggle. Instead they fell asleep—twice! Yet few of us are inclined to blame the disciples, for we know how hard it can be to persist in prayer.

Extended prayer is often the most challenging task for Christians to tackle. Carving out a block of time is the first challenge, but the second is even harder: to keep focused on the Lord for a long time. Nevertheless, we love God, and we want to learn to love Him better with our minds. So we seek His strength and set ourselves to the task He puts before us: to keep "seeking His face" even when our minds are prone to wander off for minutes at a time.

God delights to teach us how to pray, and He often uses the experiences of other Christians. In Joni Eareckson Tada's book *A Quiet Place in a Crazy World*, she shared her way of breaking up an hour of prayer into 5-minute blocks: praise, waiting, and so on.[4] Inspired, I wrote her list on a card and added time notations for the hour and half hour—as printed here on the page. How helpful this tool has been for keeping on track in some of my own prayer times! I place the card beside me, often reset the clock a bit, and start praying. Sometimes I'm speaking; sometimes I'm quiet; sometimes my eyes are closed; sometimes I'm looking at sections of scripture to use for prayer; sometimes I'm singing from a songbook. I more or less follow the topics on the card, but I remember that it's there to help me—not a task master, but a tool. If I pray "past" a certain topic, I either go back or skip it. If my mind wanders—usually when I've stopped speaking out loud—then the card gives me a way to jump back into prayer.

00	Praise	30
05	Waiting	35
10	Confession	40
15	Scripture praying	45
20	Watching	50
25	Interceding	55
30	Petitioning	00
35	Thanksgiving	05
40	Singing	10
45	Meditating	15
50	Listening	20
55	Praise	25

33

> O Lord, who may abide in Your tent? Who may dwell on Your holy hill? He who walks with integrity, and works righteousness, and speaks truth in his heart. He does not slander with his tongue, nor does evil to his neighbor, nor takes up a reproach against his friend . . . . (Ps. 15:1-3)

When we look beyond the beautiful poetry in this psalm, those of us who love the Lord may sigh. We want to dwell on His holy hill, to abide in His tent—in short, to stay as close to the Lord as He'll let us.

But ah, our hearts! Sometimes I've managed to act kindly to a difficult person and speak nothing but encouraging words, yet the very slander I *didn't* speak plays itself over and over inside me. This state of affairs doesn't surprise God, and He wants me to know the truth of the matter as well: "The heart is more deceitful than all else and is desperately sick; who can understand it? I, the Lord, search the heart, I test the mind . . ." (Jer. 17:9-10).

Yes, ugly thoughts will come into our hearts and minds. Whether they are from our memories, from our creative imagination, or directly from the Evil One, there is one appropriate response: to reject them immediately, and speak truth to our hearts. "No, no, I will not slander my brother in my heart. Lord, I will honor You in my attitude toward Martin, and I ask You to give him Your wisdom and strength. Thank You for Your good plans for him."

Dwelling on God's holy hill for extended periods of time, to love and worship and serve, requires the regular swatting away of sinful thoughts. This is normal. We can handle it, because "His divine power has given us everything we need for life and godliness through the knowledge of Him who called us" (2 Pet. 1:3).

34

> Our fathers were all under the cloud and all passed through the sea; and all were baptized into Moses in the cloud and in the sea; and all ate the same spiritual food; and all drank the same spiritual drink, for they were drinking from a spiritual rock which followed them; and the rock was Christ. (1 Cor. 10:1-4)

One day I was meditating on the metaphor of Christ the Rock, and I thought of a rock above the surface of a stormy sea, and myself trying to cling to it. "You'd never last," I told myself scornfully. "You'd only be able to hold on for a few seconds, and then you'd have to let go."

Then the thought came: what if I were stronger? And I remembered what had happened just that morning. Six weeks earlier I had begun (from ground zero) a daily regimen of strength, endurance, and flexibility exercises. Aging knees had forced me to give up my favorite fitness activities, and the best advice available recommended building up the surrounding muscle groups so that I could—eventually—safely try cycling. My new long workout was boring—no musical accompaniment, as I would lose count of repetitions; it was initially painful, even after I halved my original unambitious plans; and it was depressing to compare this tedium with the aerobic fun I had once enjoyed.

My least favorite new exercise, one for strengthening hamstrings, required holding my body in a sitting position with my back against a wall. "Slowly work your way up to two minutes," said the instructions. This half-squat had started out by being excruciating, and I could only manage ten seconds. But that morning a surprising thing occurred: thirty seconds passed before my legs told me they felt any stress at all! I was amazed, and did a check to make sure I was actually in the correct position.

What in the world had happened? Apparently, I'd gotten stronger. Inch by inch, imperceptibly from my own perspective, I'd gone from being an absolute weakling to being a physically stronger person.

"Be strong . . . !" We love God by honoring His commands to be strong, and this may include resolutely sticking to some routines that have become tedious or inconvenient yet undeniably "build us up on our most holy faith," as Jude put it. If we're not strong, we need to be doing what it takes to get that way, and continue doing what it takes to stay that way.

Strong enough to cling to the Rock of our salvation, the source of our strength, and *never* let go!

35

> O Israel, if you would listen to Me! . . . I, the Lord, am your God, who brought you up from the land of Egypt; open your mouth wide and I will fill it . . . . Oh, that My people would listen to Me, that Israel would walk in My ways! . . . I would feed you with the finest of the wheat, and with honey from the rock I would satisfy you. (Ps. 81:8-16)

Parents understand the deep concern and frustration of raising a child who won't eat properly. When the child becomes older, they can try logic, threats, or bribery to get their offspring to swallow a small amount of the healthy vegetables. But a baby simply closes its mouth.

Our heavenly Father experiences similar feelings with His children. He demonstrated His love for the Israelites by releasing them from slavery in Egypt, rescuing them miraculously from their pursuers by parting the Red Sea, and giving them visible proof of His presence on a 24-hour basis (cloud by day, fire by night). Yet they eventually complained about the food that appeared supernaturally every morning. "We remember the fish which we used to eat free in Egypt, the cucumbers and the melons and the leeks and the onions and the garlic, but now our appetite is gone. There is nothing at all to look at except this manna" (Num. 11:5-6).

Many passages in scripture show us that bread and manna and honey are also pictures of the rich, nutritious, and sometimes sweet wisdom that God wants to fill us up with. "Oh, that My people would listen to Me, that Israel would walk in My ways!" Our Father yearns for us to draw close and open our hearts as wide as we would open our mouths for food.

I encourage you to answer God's deep love with all your mind. Don't wander off impatiently and seek your own sweet mental snacks. Draw near and listen. This is food indeed.

> The law of the Lord is perfect, restoring the soul . . . . The precepts of the Lord are right, rejoicing the heart . . . sweeter also than honey and the drippings of the honeycomb. (Ps. 19:7-8, 10)

36

> On exactly the tenth day of this seventh month is the day of atonement; it shall be a holy convocation for you, and you shall humble your souls and present an offering by fire to the Lord. You shall not do any work on this same day . . . . It is to be a sabbath of complete rest to you, and you shall humble your souls; on the ninth of the month at evening, from evening until evening you shall keep your sabbath. (Lev. 23:27-28, 32)

Vacations and holidays are something that modern Christians understand. We need play to balance work, we need fresh experience to give us new perspectives, we need extended times for family excursions. Sabbath rests for humbling our souls are something different—and something less common among Christians. Sundays are often anything but restful.

The exciting metaphor in Isaiah 40:31 about mounting up with wings like eagles is not depicting God's people in general. Rather, it describes "those who wait for the Lord" or "wait upon the Lord." Quiet periods of waiting—in prayer, in meditation on the scriptures, in an attitude of listening attention—are one form of resting, of humbling our souls. We need to do this because our usual work, no matter how enjoyable or godly, distracts us from hearing Jesus. Whether our work involves people, information, or machines, it demands a degree of our attention. One really does need to sit (or stand or lie) quietly to hear Jesus well, so Lazarus' sister Mary was right to plunk herself down at Jesus' feet to make sure she heard every word. Jesus loved Mary's sister Martha too, and He helped her understand that her well-intentioned busyness was keeping her from the most important business of all: communing with Himself, the guest of honor.

Christians who are waiting might seem to be doing very little, but they are actually doing several things. First, they are deliberately *not* setting off to do their usual work, continue a journey, or carry forward a project. Second, they are waiting to see what the Lord will show them or teach them. These two things nourish a third, humility; each waiter acknowledges that his or her own desire to get on with things, to move forward with the activities on the agenda, is taking second place to an extended meeting with the Lord of Life. And this arrangement is as it should be, as it must be, if the Lord and the waiter are to be on the same road together at the end of the day.

David's words illustrate the love relationship we are striving for: "My soul clings to You; Your right hand upholds me" (Ps. 63:8).

37

In the dense urban sprawl of Taipei, Taiwan, I used to notice that if I passed by my neighborhood bus stop at around four in the afternoon, I would always see a certain woman waiting there on the crowded sidewalk. She was quite an ordinary woman in her forties, but she stood out because of the expression on her face. Her eyes were alert, and there was an intentness about her that seemed out of place for someone merely awaiting a bus. One day the mystery was solved and I saw something I have never forgotten.

Just as I came on the scene, a bus pulled up, sardine-can-packed with school students in their blue uniforms, the regulation book-bags with the long straps slung over their shoulders. Among the tall children who unpacked themselves and alighted was a teenage girl who instantly smiled and walked toward the woman (clearly her mother), who moved forward to meet her. The two immediately fell into conversation, and as they moved away from the crowd and up the street, in one smooth movement the mother took the heavy book-bag onto her right shoulder as the daughter simultaneously slipped it from her left one. The transfer was so flawless it might have been choreographed. No protests on the strong young girl's part, nothing breaking the rhythm of their obviously happy talk. The vignette was complete when the girl slung an arm around her mother's shoulders.

Jesus said, "Come to Me, all who are weary and heavy-laden, and I will give you rest. Take My yoke upon you and learn from Me, for I am gentle and humble in heart, and you will find rest for your souls. For My yoke is easy and My burden is light" (Matt. 11:28-30). This well-known teaching is full of paradoxes. Weary people are promised rest, yet they're also promised that there will still be a burden to carry. On the other hand, they are offered the chance to walk in harness with Jesus—like two oxen together—and learn how to carry it.

Love the Lord by letting Him show you how to use your strength: not as if you were a single pack donkey, but as if you were one of two oxen. Let the Lord direct you when to tug with all your might, and when to let up a bit. And sometimes you may find a heavy load has slipped off your shoulders onto His.

38

> In six days the Lord made the heavens and the earth, the sea and all that is in them, and rested on the seventh day; therefore the Lord blessed the sabbath day and made it holy. (Ex. 20:11)

Very few societies in the world take one full day out of a week to desist from their own work, their own pleasures, and their own words in order to do nothing but delight in God. Christians who live in cultures that extol the virtue of diligence may drive themselves even harder than those around them, striving to give their best efforts to their jobs, their families, their church. Pastors and church workers are often the most weary and heavy-laden; their congregations expect (and these ministers may agree) that those in "fulltime ministry" should be ready to forego regular rest days to accomplish God's work; and this lack of rest becomes the pattern of their lives.

Perhaps part of our disobedience to the "rest" commands in the scriptures stems from the way we read the accounts of Jesus' ministry. As soon as Jesus returns from His forty days of wilderness testing, He begins training disciples, teaching, and healing. The Father keeps the Son busy (John 5:19 indicates that the Son is carrying out directives), and the ministry is set to end in just three years. We read that Jesus sometimes went off alone to pray; but we also read that once when He and His disciples were unsuccessful in escaping the crowds, Jesus went ahead and continued ministering to them. We realize that the four gospel accounts don't give us enough detail—we are given key events and teachings, not "a typical day in the life of Jesus." Yet we still find ourselves paying more attention to what the narratives tell us Jesus *did*, rather than to what Jesus commanded *us* to do.

Jesus said that He came to fulfill the Law, not to abolish it. And Jesus tells us that life under His yoke will include rest, because His yoke and load are not heavy. His load is not like the loads we agree to let others strap onto us, and not like the loads we lay on ourselves to impress others. His load is one that only a gentle, humble servant will be able to carry properly. He will teach us this gentleness and humility. And He will show us when to rest and do nothing but delight in God.

39

> Bless the Lord, O my soul, and all that is within me, bless His holy name. Bless the Lord, O my soul, and forget none of His benefits. (Ps. 103:1-2)

When God has just done a wonderful thing in our lives, our souls burst with praise. The first chapter of Luke records Mary's joyful acknowledgement that she is pregnant with the son of God, and her first words are, "My soul exalts the Lord." Exodus 15 records the ecstatic song Moses and the Israelites sang when their mighty God parted the Red Sea. Certainly in those moments, God's people were loving Him with all their souls.

But as time passes, a powerful experience of God's presence and work in our lives can become a distant memory. Events we thought we would never forget are crowded out by more recent concerns. Our souls don't leap within us to give the Lord spontaneous worship and praise.

So our souls need to be taken in hand. David models this in the psalm above. He commands his soul "and all that is within me" to bless God. He reminds himself that it is God "who pardons all your iniquities, who heals all your diseases; who redeems your life from the pit, who crowns you with lovingkindness and compassion; who satisfies your years with good things, so that your youth is renewed like the eagle" (vv. 3-5).

We, too, can take our souls in hand and tell them to join all creation in blessing God fully. And to get ourselves started, we can deliberately remind ourselves of the benefits God has poured out on us in past weeks, months, and years. The Jews had the records in scripture to remind them of God's past dealings with them. We too can make records in journals of special ways the Lord has worked in our lives.

Then in times of dryness or doubt, we can reread what we have written, and recall even more details. And as we read, we can bless the Lord with all that is within us.

40

> How precious to me are your thoughts, O God! How vast is the sum of them! Were I to count them, they would outnumber the grains of sand. When I awake, I am still with you. (Ps. 139:17-18 NIV)

Like many Christians, I'm regularly amazed when I read Psalm 139. It reminds me of how closely and how well God knows me. He knows me not just because He created me, but because He is constantly *there*, looking at me from the inside out. "You know when I sit down and when I rise; you perceive my thoughts from afar. You discern my going out and my lying down; you are familiar with all my ways (Ps. 139:2-3 NIV).

Not only does God know us, He loves us, and He constantly comes near to us to nudge, speak, remind, and direct us. Throughout this morning, I was aware of a fraction of His uncountable thoughts toward me: as I fashioned two of His lessons to me to share with others in this daily devotional; as I turned to my freelance test-writing work and saw ideas pop into my mind to meet the demands of the assignment; as I played a song on the piano and realized that this was something my little goddaughter might enjoy learning, an activity we could enjoy together; as I wondered how to connect with another little girl far away and suddenly came across a postcard featuring sharks, her favorite animal. And as I washed the breakfast dishes, and walked along city streets, and negotiated transfers in the subway stations, God dropped insights into my mind about relationships with friends and family members, about classes I'm teaching, about simple things to remember to do.

Little children learn the language of family love from their parents—they hug and kiss, first by rote and later with joyful abandon. As children of our Father in heaven, we can strive to copy His own expressions of His love toward us. We can pause throughout our day—and ask the Holy Spirit to remind us to pause—to turn our thoughts to God. We love Him with our minds as we do this. "Thank You, Lord, for the way this task is being accomplished . . . . Thank You for the patience You're giving me with this person . . . . Oh, Lord, I'm sorry. Thank You for setting me straight on this . . . . Lord, help me not to make a decision too quickly here . . . ."

> Teach me to do Your will, for You are my God; let Your good Spirit lead me on level ground. (Ps. 143:10)

41

> Make me know Your ways, O Lord; teach me Your paths. Lead me in Your truth and teach me, for You are the God of my salvation; for You I wait all the day. (Ps. 25:4-5)

> Examine me, O Lord, and try me; test my mind and my heart. For Your lovingkindness is before my eyes, and I have walked in Your truth. (Ps. 26:2-3)

David's beautiful, passionate prayers sound wonderful when read aloud in a church service. But how can we "wait all the day" on God when there are essays to correct, clients to meet with? How do I keep God's lovingkindness "before my eyes" when I'm not sitting alone with my Bible open?

When we truly want to honor God, to love Him by the ways we think and act, He answers our prayers for guidance and correction. And we can do a few things to make sure we hear His answers. We can avoid keeping our minds so occupied with trivia that we miss His words to us. We can also deliberately eject sinful thoughts (such as lust, fear, jealousy, hatred) that have no business taking up residence in our minds.

Even in the midst of busy days, there is space around the edges for the Holy Spirit to give counsel. If we drop the habit of filling "down time" by checking our email or making a phone call, there is even more space. God *loves* to teach us His ways. He shows me that the judgment I was making about my friend's critical nature is as a piece of sawdust compared to the impatience I just acted out with the slow gentleman in front of me on the escalator. He shows me that my true reason for dividing up the discussion group the way I did was not the natural, sensible reason apparent to everyone but rather my prejudice against one of the members—and this was an intention I had managed to hide even from myself.

And the more I learn to say "no" to thoughts that have no business in my mind, the more the Holy Spirit is there—correcting, directing, reminding, leading me into loving thoughts and small actions of love toward others.

> Behold, You desire truth in the innermost being, and in the hidden part You will make me know wisdom. (Ps. 51:6)

42

> I will extol You, my God, O King; and I will bless Your name forever and ever. Every day I will bless You, and I will praise Your name forever and ever. Great is the Lord, and greatly to be praised; and His greatness is unsearchable.... I will meditate on the glorious splendor of Your majesty, and on Your wonderful works. (Ps. 145:1-3, 5)

Sooner or later, most Christians discover that meditating on and saying or singing aloud the psalms of praise in scripture does something to their spirits. It takes them closer to an infinite God whose greatness is certainly "unsearchable" yet not unapproachable. And the scriptures are full of the reminder, the directive, the command: praise Him, praise Him, praise Him!

We can partially understand the effect that praise has on our spirits by considering a magnifying glass. At a distance, a butterfly is seen as a flash of color and motion; when it lights on a nearby bush, we can appreciate the brilliant design on its wings; under a child's magnifying glass, the wings would be revealed as three-dimensional marvels of pattern and texture; and the deeper magnification of a laboratory microscope would expose mysteries once undreamed of.

"O magnify the Lord with me, and let us exalt His name together" (Ps. 34:3). When we magnify the Lord, we are acknowledging His greatness, both to Him and to ourselves. Our offerings of praise to Him honor and bless Him. Meanwhile, as the praises resound within us, they bring every other concern in our minds into correct perspective: God is the Creator of the awesome universe, the Mighty One who continues to work miracles, the God whose love will never cease to sustain us, the God who brought us naked into the world and will take us naked out of it. He is the God who has carried us for months and years, who has been faithful more times than we can remember, times we wish we had written down so that we *could* remember them.

When Jesus rode into Jerusalem on a donkey,

> the whole crowd of the disciples began to praise God joyfully with a loud voice for all the miracles which they had seen,

shouting: "Blessed is the king who comes in the name of the Lord; peace in heaven and glory in the highest!" Some of the Pharisees in the crowd said to Him, "Teacher, rebuke Your disciples." But Jesus answered, "I tell you, if these become silent, the stones will cry out!" (Luke 19:37-40).

Let's not be outdone by the stones.

43

> Jesus said to him a third time, "Simon, son of John, do you love me?" Peter was grieved because He said to him a third time, "Do you love me?" And he said to Him, "Lord, You know all things; You know that I love you." Jesus said to him, "Tend My sheep." (John 21:17)

Chapter 21 of John records the familiar story of Jesus asking Peter three times whether he loves Him, and people often draw a parallel with the three times that Peter denied knowing Jesus (John 18). They believe Jesus was reassuring Peter that he was forgiven and accepted as a disciple and servant. But the original Greek language of the scripture teaches us another lesson about the love of God. It turns out that the quality of love Jesus was asking for was greater than what Peter was prepared to offer. Two different Greek words for "love" were used. The dialog actually went like this:

Jesus: Simon, do you *love me unconditionally*? (agapao)
Peter: Master, you know I *have affection for you*. (phileo)
Jesus: Tend my lambs . . . Simon, do you love me unconditionally? (agapao)
Peter: Yes, Lord; you know that I have affection for you. (phileo)
Jesus: Shepherd my sheep . . . Simon, do you have affection for me? (phileo)
Peter: Lord, you know all things; You know that I have affection for you. (phileo)
Jesus: Tend my sheep.

Jesus begins by asking Peter for the high-wide-deep-strong "agapao" or "agape" love that is used throughout the New Testament narratives and letters to describe God's amazing love. Jesus asks twice for this "agape" love, and each time Peter can only offer affection. The surprise ending is that the third time Jesus steps down to Peter's level and uses Peter's own language of love.

The Lord loves us deeply and knows us well. He wants to continually draw us further into a participation in His huge, limitless love. Meanwhile, He tells us to serve Him and the family of God with the love we have gotten hold of so far.

44

Now the God of peace . . . equip you in every good thing to do His will, working in us that which is pleasing in His sight, through Jesus Christ . . . . (Heb. 13:20-21)

Consider it all joy, my brethren, when you encounter various trials, knowing that the testing of your faith produces endurance. And let endurance have its perfect result, so that you may be perfect and complete, lacking in nothing. (James 1:2-4)

For several months, I worked as a nurse's aide in a skilled care facility, assisting residents with their dressing, bathing, and meals. The work was physically demanding, and sometimes assisting heavy patients meant finding another team member to help. When coming onto a shift, aides always checked the roster to find out who was "on" with them. How encouraging it was to see certain names—he or she was so strong and capable, so willing to help out! (Seeing names such as my own just brought a shrug—names of folks who tried hard, but just didn't have what it took.)

Physical muscles can be built in a gym. Spiritual muscles are built as we encounter various trials and endure, endure, endure. We agree to endure because this is God's way of equipping us to be on His team of aides. But the real meaning of having "spiritual muscles" is that we have more of Jesus in us. It isn't that we just "seem" more like Christ to others, so that they (and we) are tempted to admire the likeness. It's that the love coming forth from us is Jesus' own powerful love: comforting, healing, exhorting, bringing light and wisdom.

Just as we still love God with an imperfect love—the quality of love we've gotten hold of thus far—so our love for others is limited. Yet the more of Christ's likeness that is developed in us, built into us, the more love we will have to pour out on those God gives us to serve. And that is why we are asked to consider the trials "all joy."

45

> Love is patient, love is kind . . . [it] does not rejoice in unrighteousness, but rejoices with the truth; bears all things, believes all things, hopes all things, endures all things."
> (1 Cor. 13:4-7)

For many years, I was regularly entangled in a chronic sin which greatly limited my usefulness as a servant of God. Of course, any unconfessed sin can take root in our hearts and (sooner or later) poison our relationship with God and others. But fault-finding, or judgment, was a sin I carried around with me like a suicide-bomber; I exploded without warning among friends, among strangers, or in meetings with criticisms, complaints, dissatisfied expressions, subtle finger-pointing, and slander.

My greatest anger was directed at Christian friends who acted in ways that were unjust and unloving toward others or myself. (Yes, I saw the irony of this as clearly as readers will, but it didn't dissipate the anger.) And when I saw a repeated offense, I would congratulate myself on noticing that "there he goes again!"

I have written the above in the past tense of English grammar, yet in truth I am still learning love's lesson. Like Paul, I still only "know in part." If I fully comprehended the immense love of God for all those He created, all of us who turn our backs and shut our ears to Him again and again, I would no longer be struggling.

> I [God] took them in My arms; but they did not know that I healed them. I led them with cords of a man, with bonds of love, and I became to them as one who lifts the yoke from their jaws; and I bent down and fed them. (Hos. 11:3-4)

Love hopes all things. It hopes for an openness, to see evidence that God is already at work under a hard heart. (Under a heart as hard as our own has sometimes been.) It hopes to see some good, some light, in the darkness of this person who was made in God's image.

Pursue love.

46

> Let me hear Your lovingkindness in the morning; for I trust in You. Teach me the way in which I should walk; for to You I lift up my soul. (Ps. 143:8)

> The Sovereign Lord . . . wakens me morning by morning, wakens my ear to listen like one being taught. The Sovereign Lord has opened my ears, and I have not been rebellious; I have not drawn back. (Is. 50:4-5 NIV)

In the book of Psalms, David's writings indicate that waking and waiting for God's instructions was a way of life for him. Scripture records that David committed both adultery and murder but that he was also "a man after God's own heart." The passage above from the book of Isaiah is presumed to be prophetic, describing Jesus, but its truth surely also applies to those who (as David did) seek God with all their hearts.

God desires to speak to us. "He wakens my ear to listen as a disciple." Are we able to hear Him?

Some mornings, I wake up with my brain doing replays of recent input—the plot of a detective novel, scenes from a movie, events that happened in class last evening. And sometimes, to my surprise, God gives me an insight out of the seemingly "secular" clutter: a truth about Himself and His ways, or about people, about me, about His world.

Some mornings, I deliberately turn to God as soon as consciousness comes and ask if there is anything He wants to say. If there is time, I lie there for awhile and sing whatever comes to my tongue. Perhaps if I waited longer before opening my own mouth, I'd hear His words more often (and they are usually impressions or "inner words").

How can we discern God's voice when our minds are so cluttered with other thoughts? My father once took me to a section of woods in which the trees grew quite close together; he wanted me to hear the amazingly loud cacophony of hundreds of birds, and not all of the same species. At one point, he tried to direct my attention to one particular bird's call: "Listen, do you hear that?" I had to admit I couldn't hear the call he described, even when he imitated it for me and had me listen again.

But Dad could hear it. Through practice he could hear it distinctly. And so will we, through practice, learn to hear our Father's voice.

47

> "If anyone hears My voice and opens the door, I will come in to him and will dine with him, and he with Me." (Rev. 3:20)

A recent trip back to America to visit my mother led to some new reflections on Revelation 3:20 and on loving God with my mind.

After getting my luggage checked in for the night flight, I found an airport restaurant and settled down to a huge bowl of nourishing-looking vegetable noodle soup. As I ate it, I thanked God quietly for how calm He had kept me through the whole packing process, through getting my work finished at the office, through the taxi ride in the Friday evening traffic. Just then, an unsavory thought popped into my mind, triggered by something I noticed nearby. As I immediately ejected the thought, I found myself thinking, "Goodness, yes, we certainly don't need to discuss *that* at the dinner table."

Then I smiled, because that was what I had been doing over my bowl of soup: dining with my Lord. The image in scripture is such an apt one. I had been sitting and consciously ruminating over the day's affairs and enjoying Jesus' presence at the table as much as I was enjoying the warm steam coming up from the tall bowl. And His presence made me quickly recognize that ugly, dishonorable thoughts dishonored my Guest (and Host) at the table.

During the pleasant 10-day visit with Mom at her retirement center, I reflected again on the dining experience. Mom had a regular table in the dining hall, so three times a day we sat with a delightful couple named Warren and LaVerne. Fortunately, they were as chatty as I, so we had lively exchanges about our ideas and experiences, life's little things and bigger things too. Looking back, I spent *hours* with them. I didn't get to know any of Mom's other friends nearly as well, because these two were the ones we had our meals with.

Paul wrote the Thessalonian church to "pray without ceasing," and I used to wonder how in the world such a command could be obeyed. Now I see that a person can start by dining with Jesus. By practicing long, lazy periods of hanging out with Him. And food can help—you start out by thanking Him and then just leave off the "Amen." And as you eat, keep right on communicating.

48

> Good and upright is the Lord; therefore He instructs sinners in the way. He leads the humble in justice, and He teaches the humble His way. (Ps. 25:8-9)

When God did a marvelous thing in the family of a woman named Gweihua, other friends and I encouraged her to write it up for a Christian magazine, where it would surely bless thousands of others. Gweihua, a naturally shy person, responded in dismay, "No! I'm too meek!" To this I replied, "Good! Because God will be able to work with you."

The scriptures both tell us and show us that the humble are God's favorite people. Jesus said, "Blessed are the poor (or humble, or meek) in spirit, for theirs is the kingdom of heaven" (Matt. 5:3). And God frequently carries out His work using men and women whom anyone, themselves included, would consider inadequate for their missions.

God chose Moses, who was so "slow of speech and slow of tongue" that he begged God to be let off speaking to the Egyptian ruler. To create "a great nation" which would bless "all the families of the earth," God called 75-year-old Abraham and fulfilled His plans through Abraham's aged wife Sarah. Gideon, who became known as God's mighty warrior, was the youngest member of the smallest family of the Mannaseh tribe. Saul, before becoming king, was another "least of the least." David was a young shepherd. Joseph was Jacob's favored son, but he spent years in slavery and prison before God called him for His special task.

Because these chosen ones had a humble attitude toward their own abilities and credentials, because they felt they didn't deserve the authority and responsibility being given to them, God could effectively put them in exalted positions. Some would eventually fall through allowing their *hearts* to become exalted as well, but for a time they would faithfully, humbly carry out their enormous responsibilities. They would remember they were servants, not little gods.

How can we maintain faithful, loving hearts that don't become exalted? By keeping our eyes on Jesus. "Have this attitude in yourselves which was also in Christ Jesus, who, although He existed in the form of God, did not regard equality with God a thing to be grasped, but emptied Himself, taking the form of a bond-servant . . . . He humbled Himself by becoming obedient to the point of death, even death on a cross" (Phil. 2:5-8).

49

The plans of the heart belong to man, but the answer of the tongue is from the Lord. (Prov. 16:1)

The mind of man plans his way, but the Lord directs his steps. (Prov. 16:9)

When we are constantly reaching out with our minds and hearts toward God, He enables us to make wise decisions in our lives; thus "our" plans are certainly ours, but we trust we are walking along a path He has opened to us. We recognize that the path might take an unexpected turn, so we remain poised for new developments.

I was recently asked to meet with two colleagues from a branch office on a writing project I would be doing for them. I had prayed about taking on the work, felt it was right to move ahead, and expected that God would give me all the inspiration needed for the task. As one of the colleagues was a former close associate and the other a very junior colleague, the meeting was relaxed and casual; and I expressed quite naturally my expectation that God would provide me with good ideas. My friend grinned and said, "Well, you and Marsha will have a lot to talk about."

"Oh, are you a Christian too?" The conversation turned, and I learned that Marsha was a member of one of the groups that borrow Christian truths and then move off into a manmade religion. I couldn't remember the details about where this group's teachings veered away from those of scripture, but Marsha and I had a short discussion about some things in the Bible, and I made some comments about the excellent translations now available and the easy access to interlinear reference texts.

I later learned that the subjects I had "happened" to bring up were some of those which Marsha's church had the most flawed understanding of. I believed that these "answers of the tongue" were indeed from the Lord—for Marsha, with love. And I marveled that such a conversation had ever begun, or continued, in a job setting. The experience made me more eager than ever to have the Lord direct my steps.

50

> What man among you, if he has a hundred sheep and has lost one of them, does not leave the ninety-nine in the open pasture and go after the one which is lost until he finds it? When he has found it, he lays it on his shoulder, rejoicing. And when he comes home, he calls together his friends and neighbors, saying to them, "Rejoice with me, for I have found my sheep which was lost!" I tell you that in the same way, there will be more joy in heaven over one sinner who repents than over ninety-nine righteous persons who need no repentance. (Luke 15:4-7)

Jesus follows this parable with the one in which the woman searches carefully for her lost coin, and He repeats that "there is joy in the presence of the angels of God over one sinner who repents." Then comes the parallel tale known as "the prodigal son" (Luke 15:11-32).

How many of us have felt that the emphasis on the missing hundredth sheep seemed out of proportion? We didn't suppose Jesus meant the ninety-nine in the "open pasture" had been abandoned or left exposed to danger; but perhaps by our standards it seemed unfair that the angels didn't, and don't, seem to care much about the other ninety-nine sheep. About *us*.

And yet they do. Of course they do. And so does God. But loving God means learning to know His heart, learning to love as He loves. Paul prays for Christians that "the eyes of your heart may be enlightened, that you will know what is the hope of His calling, what are the riches of the glory of His inheritance in the saints, and what is the surpassing greatness of His power toward us who believe" (Eph. 1:18-19). With that enlightened knowledge, we can never doubt the boundless love that Father God has toward us.

The elder son in the parable of the prodigal son refuses to join the party for his forgiven, restored brother because he has never understood his father's heart. "His father came out and began pleading with him, but to no avail." So the father tries to explain. And the words in Jesus' parable teach us who we are as God's children, and what principles our Father wants implanted deep in our hearts:

> "But we had to celebrate and rejoice, for this brother of yours was dead, and has begun to live" (Luke 15:31-32).

God's children need to strive for a maturity that gets them standing alongside the Father and accepting the "we." Then they too will be sorrowing for the lost, seeking the lost, and joining in wild celebration for those born or restored to new life.

51

> The Jews were marveling, saying, "How has this man become learned, having never been educated?" Jesus therefore answered them, and said, "My teaching is not Mine, but His who sent Me. If any man is willing to do His will, he shall know of the teaching, whether it is of God, or whether I speak from Myself. (John 7:15-17)

I expect that nearly everyone using these devotional readings as a tool to love God more fully is a Christian. The gospel of John describes Christians as those who have received Jesus and been given the right—by Jesus, not by a particular church—to become children of God; those who have gone through the mystery of being "born of God" (John 1:12-13). Jesus Himself describes this spiritual event as being born again, or born from above, or born of the Spirit (John 3:3-8).

If you are not a Christian, but desire more than anything to love and obey God, Jesus' promise above is for you. You can ask God to show you whether Jesus' teachings and claims about Himself are true.

Ask God about Jesus' words: "He has given all judgment to the Son, in order that all may honor the Son, even as they honor the Father. He who does not honor the Son does not honor the Father who sent Him" (John 5:22-23). "This is the will of My Father, that everyone who beholds the Son and believes in Him, may have eternal life; and I Myself will raise him up on the last day" (John 6:40).

God knows us, sees us, examines our heart's attitude toward Him. When our heart's desire is to obey Him, He pours out the wisdom we need.

Christians, add your prayers to mine today for the seekers reading this book. When we do this, we are adding to Jesus' own prayer on His last night with the disciples: "I do not ask in behalf of these alone, but for those who believe in Me through their word; that they may all be one, even as You, Father, are in Me, and I in You, that they also may be in Us; that the world may believe that You sent Me" (John 17:20-21).

52

> Give thanks to the Lord, call on His name. Make known His deeds among the peoples; make them remember that His name is exalted. Praise the Lord in song, for He has done excellent things; let this be known throughout the earth. (Is. 12:4-5)

Throughout the ages, people have found that putting words into songs is an effective way to make them memorable. Generations of children have learned songs and chants to memorize the alphabet, grammar rules, and math tables. Nowadays, advertisers make much use of this powerful memory aid, and that silly song we can't get out of our heads is what gets us buying one of their products.

It is God's people who have given songs their most glorious use: as a means to praise the Creator, to make His deeds known to everyone, to enable the singers to "remember that His name is exalted." In earlier eras, before individuals had Bibles in their homes, much of what Christians learned of God's truth was from the songs they sang Sunday after Sunday when they assembled together. In societies today where people cannot read, or where Christians are persecuted and Bibles are scarce, or where scripture translations in their languages still don't exist, songs still play their powerful role in teaching and reminding and encouraging God's people with God's truth.

Love the Lord by praising Him in song, by filling your mind and your mouth with songs that repeat wonderful truths about His nature and His promises. The great hymns of the past, as well as contemporary worship music, contain songs like this. "How Great Thou Art," one of the former, proclaims God as the mighty Creator of the wonders of nature, and as the loving Father who carried out His plan for our salvation. "The Steadfast Love of the Lord," a simple but classic contemporary chorus, puts music to Lamentations 3:22-23 and praises God for His faithful mercies, which are "new every morning."

While exciting new church music comes and goes, such songs as these live on because they speak truth to our anxious minds. As we join in the singing, our minds are crying out, "Yes, Lord, yes!"

53

> Now set your heart and your soul to seek the Lord your God . . . . (1 Chr. 22:19)

> Set your hearts unto all the words which I testify among you this day, which ye shall command your children to observe to do, all the words of this law. For it is not a vain thing for you; because it is your life . . . . (Deut. 32:46-47 KJV)

> I have set the Lord continually before me; because He is at my right hand, I will not be shaken. (Ps. 16:8)

In the modern world, we are accustomed to using machinery which can run by itself once its controls have been set. Captains of planes and ocean vessels can set their crafts on automatic pilot and take a break; drivers can set their car on cruise control and the vehicle will maintain the same speed, even when they take their foot off the pedal.

In the era when the scriptures above were spoken by Moses and David, "automatic" was not in the vocabulary of any language. Sailors would set their course with relation to the North Star or one of the constellations, and continually adjust the rigging so that the vessel remained in the proper position with reference to the heavenly lights. Horses pulling carts or chariots had to be deliberately steered and driven, urged ahead with whips when they became tired.

When we become Christians, we consciously set our hearts on following Christ. Our confession of faith in Jesus, our vow to accept Him as the Lord, the King, the Master of our lives, our water baptism—in these ways, with our hearts and our words and our actions, we were setting ourselves on a course toward a deeper knowledge and deeper love of God.

By God's mighty power and grace, when we accepted Christ our spirits came alive, spirits that can sense God's voice and directions, spirits that will live forever. However, nothing about our ensuing walk with God will ever be automatic. Sinful habits we formerly indulged in will tempt us for months, even years. Painful situations and difficult people will still be part of our lives sometimes. Daily decisions, large and seemingly small (Will I keep chewing on this thought? Or confess it as sin and send it away?), will determine whether or not we remain steadfast on course, with the Lord continually before us. Whenever we wander off course, we'll need to reset our hearts as quickly as we can.

Let's make Paul's prayer our own: "May the Lord direct your hearts into the love of God and into the steadfastness of Christ" (2 Thess. 3:5).

54

> I will give You thanks with all my heart; I will sing praises to You before the gods. I will bow down toward Your holy temple and give thanks to Your name for Your lovingkindness and Your truth; for You have magnified Your word according to all Your name. (Ps. 138:1-2)

Many societies celebrate a day of thanksgiving, sometimes related to a national event in history, sometimes in connection with a yearly harvest. Christians often seize such days as opportunities to look back and thank God for His provisions during the past year.

The Jews were taught to bring thank offerings, sacrifices specifically meant to express thanksgiving to God for His continuing care. This was a deliberate acknowledgement that blessings had been received from God, who was therefore deserving of fervent thanks; and now, at this day and time, and in this way, He would be given the thanksgiving due to Him.

Thanksgiving days are one more avenue of loving God with all our hearts. We do well to arrange gatherings with other Christians for times of sharing what God has done, and thereby multiplying the thanks God will receive for His works. Some church groups have yearly or monthly occasions for doing this, whether in big meeting halls or around a table. Such set times are helpful as "date nights" with God, times to pull away from the dozens of concerns and activities we are usually involved in, and come to a place where Jesus is the guest of honor. They are times when everything that is said gives love, honor, and thanks to Him.

> Let them give thanks to the Lord for His lovingkindness, for His wonders to the sons of men! Let them also offer sacrifices of thanksgiving, and tell of His works with joyful singing. (Ps. 107:21-22)

55

> Work out your salvation with fear and trembling; for it is God who is at work in you, both to will and to work for His good pleasure. Do all things without grumbling or disputing; so that you will prove yourselves to be blameless and innocent, children of God above reproach in the midst of a crooked and perverse generation, among whom you appear as lights in the world, holding fast to the word of life . . . . (Phil. 2:12-16)

There is a popular tendency to generalize about personality types: outgoing versus introverted, easygoing versus anxious and critical. Philosophers and psychologists have posited even more complex groupings, suggesting that each "type" has its strengths and weaknesses. However close or far a particular system is to describing the fascinating variety of humankind, and however much we value the appreciation it gives us of others' differences, there is one thing we must beware of. We must not accept a personality descriptor as a way of avoiding obedience.

I am one those people described as detail-oriented, critical, perfectionistic. I tend to get anxious when a situation doesn't match my assessment of the way things "ought to be." Then I tend to grumble and to trample on others' opinions by arguing persistently that things need to be fixed.

But scripture teaches that I am to "do all things without grumbling or disputing." And there is strength in me to obey this command because God is at work in me, both to will and to work for His good pleasure.

Loving God with my strength includes holding back a "natural tendency," even when worldly wisdom would advise me not to try, that it's just the way I am. In the final analysis, I love God by accepting *His* definitions and turn away from sin.

56

> Then the Lord came and stood and called as at other times, "Samuel! Samuel!" And Samuel said, "Speak, for Your servant is listening." (1 Sam. 3:10)

One of the most delightful stories in the Bible is one so accessible that children learn it in Sunday School. It is the account of Samuel, a young boy whose mother dedicated him to the service of God at birth. From that time, he lived with the family of Eli, the priest at Shiloh, "ministering to the Lord."

One day Samuel was taking his turn "lying down in the temple of the Lord where the ark of God was" when he heard God's voice. But he didn't know it was God. He thought it was Eli.

Perhaps the most interesting part of this account is the writer's comment earlier in the chapter: "Now Samuel did not yet know the Lord, nor had the word of the Lord yet been revealed to him" (v. 7). Samuel had been living with the family of the local priest; surely no child in the town had had more exposure to the teachings of the Torah, or to the sacrifices offered by godly believers. But the writer shows us the distinction: Samuel did not yet know God as the wonderful counselor, the God who speaks to His servants. And even when Samuel heard God's voice, he didn't realize what he had heard.

But it *was* the Lord speaking to Samuel. When Eli discerned this, he taught Samuel the right response, and from that point Samuel's ears were open and ready to hear the first of many messages that his Lord had for him.

In Psalm 139, it is clear that David has had a rich experience of the abundance of God's thoughts toward him. David writes that these thoughts are precious and uncountable, and he adds, "When I awake, I am still with You" (v. 18).

Elizabeth Alves, president of Intercessors International, has written, "Throughout the years, I have discovered that most people hear the voice of the Lord, but just don't recognize it."[5] If the Lord was with David when he went to sleep and rose up, He is certainly with us as well. As we sense His presence, we can ask in love, "Speak, Lord. I'm Your servant, and I'm listening."

57

> You are my hiding place; You preserve me from trouble; You surround me with songs of deliverance. (Ps. 32:7)

The psalms are filled with references to songs and music. We are exhorted to sing songs of praise because God is worthy of this kind of carefully fashioned, thoughtful, joyful praise: "Sing to Him a new song; play skillfully with a shout of joy. For the word of the Lord is upright; and all His work is done in faithfulness. He loves righteousness and justice; the earth is full of the lovingkindness of the Lord" (Ps. 33:3-5).

But have you noticed that the scriptures also tell us that the Lord sings to us? He does! He sings back to us songs that we already know, and He gives us new songs as well.

In the scripture above, David praises the Lord who not only preserves him from trouble but sings to David of the deliverance he is going to experience. Songs of affirmation and promise.

In Psalm 40:3, we read, "He put a new song in my mouth, a song of praise to our God." Many Christians have experienced receiving songs from God—simple ones that they might or might not share with others, and some that end up being sung by millions. Songs of praise and thanksgiving and truth.

God also gives songs to get our attention for prayer. "The Lord will command His lovingkindness in the daytime; and His song will be with me in the night, a prayer to the God of my life" (Ps. 42:8). God puts His songs into David's mind, and they are transformed into prayers that David prays back to Him.

One of the most helpful things I ever read about learning to hear God's voice was in Alves's *Becoming a Prayer Warrior*. She writes, "The Holy Spirit speaks through music. There are times in the morning when you wake up with a song on your heart, such as 'Only Believe.' Listen to the words; during the day it could be the very key you will need to build your faith and lead you to victory."[6]

Love the Lord with your mind by listening for His songs.

58

> A lazy man does not roast his prey, but the precious possession of a man is his diligence. (Prov. 12:27)

> The soul of the sluggard craves and gets nothing, but the soul of the diligent is made fat. (Prov. 13:4)

By now, it will be clear that the thrust of each devotional reading is how we can love God more fully, rather than how we can experience more satisfactory Christian lives. In other words, the lessons are about blessing God rather than being blessed ourselves.

Yet if the readings are serving their purpose, and you are loving God these days with *more* of your heart, soul, mind, and strength, you have undoubtedly experienced the marvelous boomerang effect. God has been propelling more of His love toward you so that you continually have more to send back. Your blessing God has naturally led to God's blessing you; and in this wonderful game of love boomerang, it is in both parties' interests that the mutual blessing continue.

Questions: How long will you continue to diligently pursue obedience to the two Great Commandments? What will you do when the novelty wears off, when the devotional ends?

Answers: You may not last long—unless you create a disciplined life for yourself. Without that, there will not be the inclination or energy to set and keep appointments with God for the rest of your life.

A disciplined life means regular sleeping hours, healthy eating habits, scheduled times for physical exercise and—top priority—for God. And none of the four need be seen as admirable but dreary routines. In short, disciplines are not task masters—they are servants. They serve us by making sure we get what we want most in life. A disciplined life gives us the sound, clear mind, the energetic body, and the alert spirit we want and need so that we can live from moment to moment walking in God's ways.

I'm learning that when sick, on vacation, or temporarily "off" a regular schedule, I must guard my daily disciplines as much as possible; I must watch what I feed my mind and body. The problem isn't the *occasional* snack or "decadent" meal, or poor TV show, or escape reading. It is the way that a surfeit of such things, unchecked, can cut into the disciplines.

The right amount of discipline serves us, so that we can serve God.

59

> Do not seek what you will eat and what you will drink, and do not keep worrying. For all these things the nations of the world eagerly seek; but your Father knows that you need these things. But seek His kingdom, and these things will be added to you. Do not be afraid, little flock, for your Father has chosen gladly to give you the kingdom. (Luke 12:29-32)

The "little flock" Jesus was speaking to was His disciples, and presumably they had been showing signs of anxiety. It isn't surprising that they would have concerns that their daily needs would continue to be met—scripture records that when Jesus had called the men to follow him, at least some of them walked right off their jobs.

For the disciples to be primarily concerned with having their basic needs met is completely normal, what "the nations of the world seek after." But Jesus teaches something radically different. He tells the disciples to stop worrying about these things, to stop making earning a living their first priority.

Jesus wants His disciples to trust and follow him the way that sheep trust a good shepherd and follow him with minds free of anxiety. Our Shepherd has a bigger agenda for the sheep than food, drink, and clothing, though He promises to supply these: we must "seek first His kingdom and His righteousness" (Matt. 6:33). We are to seek to know God and to honor and serve Him in the ways He is showing us, both small and large, whether or not they are related to a paycheck.

What will this mean? That will depend on God's instructions. It will certainly mean devoting hours and energy to the pursuit of Kingdom concerns. It may mean getting less sleep in order to spend more time with Jesus. It may mean having shorter work hours. It may mean taking a less tiring job so that more energy is left for other tasks. It may mean simplifying one's lifestyle so that it costs less to maintain.

Do not fear, little flock, for it is your Father's good pleasure to give you the Kingdom.

60

I have told You of my ways, and You have answered me; teach me Your statutes. Make me understand the way of Your precepts, so I will meditate on Your wonders. (Ps. 119:26-27)

Establish Your word to Your servant as that which produces reverence for You. (Ps. 119:38)

The psalmist was reading and meditating on the scriptures as a means of knowing the God who had inspired them, the God who had caused them to be written. He and God had two-way communication, and this included God showing him truths in the scriptures to contemplate. The psalmist's perspective was right on target: he utilized the scriptures as a God-given tool for seeking God with all his heart.

It is so easy to make the mistake that religious scholars made in Jesus' day and get our perspective muddled: to start thinking that the goal of reading the Bible is to become Bible experts. Jesus told those scholars, "You search the Scriptures, because you think that in them you have eternal life; and it is these that bear witness of Me; and you are unwilling to come to Me, that you may have life" (John 5:39-40). One-year (or two-year, or four-year) Bible-reading plans and scripture memory cards can be excellent tools for regular intake of God's words. However, we mustn't lose perspective by focusing on the tools and quietly congratulating ourselves (or scolding ourselves) about the speed at which we are "getting through" the Bible, or about the number of verses we have memorized so far.

God hasn't called us to be scholars (not *most* of us, anyway)—He has called us to be servants, disciples, followers. We love Him by asking Him to stay alongside us as we read so He can teach us what His commands mean for us, and show us how He wants us to connect the accounts of people in the Bible with our lives today. The psalmist sings, "Open my eyes, that I may behold wonderful things from Your law" (Ps. 119:18). It is only as the Father opens our eyes that we see how wonderful His words are.

Let's keep sight of our goal in reading the Bible: to know the Lord and His ways better and better, so that we can please Him in every respect.

61

> I joyfully concur with the law of God in the inner man, but I see a different law in the members of my body, waging war against the law of my mind . . . . (Rom. 7:22-23)

> The mind set on the Spirit is life and peace . . . and those who are in the flesh cannot please God. However, you are not in the flesh but in the Spirit, if indeed the Spirit of God dwells in you. (Rom. 8:6, 8-9)

The scriptures make it clear that we Christians aren't automatons. On the one hand, we are not creatures utterly controlled by our fallen natures; our genes and our upbringing can influence our actions, but not dictate them. On the other hand, being born again did not cancel our humanity. We can say, as Paul did, "I have the mind of Christ," because by God's grace we have the power to set our minds on the Spirit. But the tug-of-war between our fallen natures and our born-again spirits will continue until we leave our bodies on the planet.

Another challenge for Christians is that our minds don't easily grasp spiritual truths. Scripture teaches, "Keep seeking the things above, where Christ is, seated at the right hand of God. Set your mind on the things above, not on the things that are on earth" (Col. 3:1-2). As we read these verses, the earthly things (people, activities, objects) are easy to visualize, but "things above" may only bring to mind a throne in a vast blue sky. When it comes to "seeking things above," what does God want us, practically speaking, to do with ourselves?

We are given some direction in a section of scripture in which Paul (while not opposing marriage) is explaining why an unmarried person is in a better position to serve the Lord. A single person is "concerned about the things of the Lord, how he may please the Lord," how he can have "undistracted devotion to the Lord"; is concerned "that she may be holy both in body and spirit"; has interests that are not divided (1 Cor. 7:32-35).

We can learn to love God by seeing our devotion as related to an earthly marriage. I have a spouse to please, and it's Jesus. He's the head of the house. Is He pleased with the place where we live together? The way our money is being used? The activities we're involved in? The amount of time we spend alone together?

This is the intimate relationship God desires with each of us. Jesus said, "If anyone loves Me, he will keep My word; and My Father will love him, and We will come to him and make Our abode with him" (John 14:23).

62

"I have not departed from the command of His lips; I have treasured the words of His mouth more than my necessary food." (Job 23:12)

It has been wisely said that the best way to learn what is really important to you is to take a look at your check book or your credit card bills: what have you been spending your money on? But another valuable possession is our *time*, our personal 24 hours. And after time allotted to sleep and our job responsibilities, the next big "expenditure" of hours is often on meals.

Hours are devoted to getting nutrients into our digestive system, keeping our cells powered up! Most or all meals are prepared in individual homes. Food is bought, cleaned, and cooked; after the time spent consuming it, dishes and utensils must be washed and put away. Whether we find this aspect of homemaking tedious or have turned cooking into a creative outlet, minutes and hours slip away as three times a day we eat.

Moreover, a missed meal is *missed*. We are hungry, and we're sorry we didn't make time for it. (If we are deliberately fasting, we aren't sorry, but we're still hungry!) Could anything be more necessary than food?

A church elder named Hsiu tells a food story from his days in the Taiwanese army. Each evening, he and his 800 fellow soldiers were required to march into the dining hall for dinner at 6:00. After that, each man could leave whenever he had finished and was free until 7:00. Hsiu remembers always trying to be the first to leave the hall, which usually meant eating less than the other men did. By doing this, he could seize the chance to use one of the two public telephones to call his fiancé. As other men wouldn't be lined up at the booth, the couple could enjoy an unhurried chat.

After a strenuous day, the soldiers needed their nourishment, and Hsiu looked forward to his meals. But, he explained, he could bear being a bit hungry. What he could not bear was not hearing the voice of his dear one as often as possible. In the era before cell phones, this required a strategy.

Like Job, we want to treasure conversations with our dear Lord more than our "necessary food." Days are short. What will be our strategies for carving out time to have those conversations?

63

> And whenever you stand praying, forgive, if you have anything against anyone; so that your Father also who is in heaven may forgive you your transgressions. (Mark 11:25)

The prayer model Jesus gave His disciples, which churches around the world call "the Lord's prayer," contains the request "Forgive us our debts" and the claim that "we also have forgiven our debtors." As this prayer is spoken, the Holy Spirit touches many hearts to remind Christians of people they have not in fact forgiven. Yet often the pray-ers rush on to the next lines and the moment for action is lost.

Many of us develop callused hearts toward those who have wronged us. English has the phrase "to nurse a grudge," and that is precisely what we do: we feed the grudge, keep it alive and well. We don't want to forget the other's sin, or to forgive it. Do we feel safe from God's wrath because our names are written in the book of life?

Jesus preached a severe sermon on the consequences of unforgiveness. He told of a king who had cancelled a huge debt owed him by one of his slaves, repayment of which would have required the man and his family to be sold. Immediately afterwards, the recipient of this merciful generosity seized a fellow slave who owed him a small amount of money and had the man thrown into prison. The king heard of his slave's behavior. "Then summoning him, his lord said to him, 'You wicked slave, I forgave you all that debt because you entreated me. Should you not also have had mercy on your fellow slave, even as I had mercy on you?' And his lord, moved with anger, handed him over to the torturers until he should repay all that was owed him. So shall My heavenly Father also do to you, if each of you does not forgive his brother from your heart'" (Matt. 18:32-35).

Unconfessed sin inevitably leads to what scripture calls uncircumcised hearts, hard hearts, callused hearts. In many cases, unforgiveness builds layer upon layer of calluses. These Christians not only accumulate new "debts" to claim against others, but also repeatedly choose unforgiveness when old grudges come to mind. Yet not offering forgiveness means withholding love, and this puts Christians in a place where they can no longer fully participate in the love of God. "The one who hates his brother is in the darkness and walks in the darkness, and does not know where he is going because the darkness has blinded his eyes" (1 John 1:11).

For Christians in need of spiritual heart surgery, we have a healer. God says, "I dwell on a high and holy place, and also with the contrite and lowly of spirit in order to revive the spirit of the lowly and to revive the heart of the contrite" (Is. 57:15).

Choose life!

64

> As those who have been chosen of God, holy and beloved, put on a heart of compassion, kindness, humility, gentleness, and patience; bearing with one another, and forgiving each other, whoever has a complaint against anyone . . . . (Col. 3:12-13)

I wonder if anyone is blessed with such an easygoing personality—or else is so filled with the love of Christ—that nobody provokes him to anger or frustration. I myself have had cause to be continually reproved by the above portion of scripture, which specifies what "love one another" actually entails.

One afternoon I was reflecting back on what I had learned from a difficult conversation with an old friend. Our chat was years overdue, and I had initiated it in obedience to God. The end result was an improved relationship, though one that still had unresolved problems. As I waited for the subway, I took out some cards with Bible verses on them. As I was reading the verses above, God explicated them for me.

"As those who have been chosen of God, holy and beloved"—Like Jesus, the Beloved, you too are holy, devoted unto God, greatly loved by Him.

"put on a heart of compassion"—Allow your heart to feel God's love and compassion toward the person.

"kindness"—Operate in this mode.

"humility"—Know that your understanding of the other person and of the situation is probably very limited, so be careful what you say.

"gentleness"—Anything you do say must be said in all gentleness.

"patience"—Don't expect any immediate change in the other person, or even an agreement in principle.

"bearing with one another, and forgiving one another"—Expect to be doing this long term, as a way of life, in all relationships, especially in some.

God's encouragement came on the heels of my obedience to step forward in love, rather than backward in fear of confrontation. As we take courage, trust God, and obey His commands, the reward is increased communication from Him. Or perhaps our obedience has made our hearts more able to hear Him.

65

> Bless the Lord, O my soul, and forget none of His benefits; who pardons all your iniquities, who heals all your diseases; who redeems your life from the pit, who crowns you with lovingkindness and compassion; who satisfies your years with good things, so that your youth is renewed like the eagle. (Ps. 103:2-5)

When the prophet Elijah was taken up into heaven, his mantle, or cloak, fell from his shoulders. It was taken up by Elisha, the younger prophet whom God had chosen to carry on Elijah's powerful prophetic ministry. "Now when the sons of the prophets who were at Jericho opposite saw him, they said, 'The spirit of Elijah rests on Elisha'" (2 Kings 2:15). Thus, today we speak of being given or passed "the mantle of responsibility."

Psalm 103 above has a glorious list of the benefits that the Lord pours out on those who love Him. But it took the Holy Spirit to show me that one of the blessings is also a mantle of responsibility. "Lovingkindness" is used throughout the psalms and other scriptures to describe something God bestows on His people. But here lovingkindness is described as a crown. According to my scholar friend, the crown is one which a queen would wear; the queen has authority because of her relationship to the king.

"Bless the Lord . . . who crowns you with lovingkindness and compassion." God crowns His people with the power and mandate to show lovingkindness and mercy to others. We are the heirs of God's marvelous grace; we are His representatives on earth. Our authority is awesome, but our mandate is limited to that which bestows God's grace on those around us.

Forgiveness can seem very hard sometimes. When it does, let's remember who we are, and whose crown we wear; whose mercies we are freely extending to others who don't deserve them; whose mercies we ourselves continue to receive, we who never deserved them either.

66

> Now Jesus said to them, "These are My words which I spoke to you while I was still with you, that all things which are written about Me in the Law of Moses and the Prophets and the Psalms must be fulfilled." Then he opened their minds to understand the Scriptures, and He said to them, "Thus it is written that the Christ would suffer and rise again from the dead the third day, and that repentance for forgiveness of sins would be proclaimed in His name to all the nations, beginning from Jerusalem." (Luke 24: 44-47)

The scriptures Jesus was talking about were written centuries before our time, in a language most of us aren't familiar with, and in historical and cultural contexts quite foreign to our experience. Because of these gaps, many Christians depend on scholars to explain the Bible to them. Linguistic and historical experts would seem to have the best tools to unlocking the meanings of the words and the events described in the Biblical narratives.

Yet even scholars who were 2000 years closer to the time when those Old Testament scriptures were written—the scholars of Jesus' time—apparently had enormous gaps in their comprehension of the writings of Moses, the prophets, and the psalms. Jesus told them that they had entirely missed the gist of the texts they had spent a lifetime studying; they had not recognized that "it is these that testify about Me" (John 5:39).

The scholars of Jesus' day were not stubbornly ignoring entire sections of scripture, sentences that were right there in the text. In the conversation with the disciples above, when Jesus says "it is written," He is not quoting an actual passage of scripture. Rather, He is *interpreting* words that God has given His people through several prophets. The scholars would never have come up with these truths themselves. Only God could reveal it to them.

Jesus tells the scholars what they lack: "I know you, that you do not have the love of God in yourselves" (John 5:42).

We love God with our minds when we turn to Him to teach us how to understand the passages of scriptures we are reading. No matter how many commentaries and other reference books we consult, we must honor God by letting Him be the Master Teacher. We can expect Him to open our minds to truths we have never seen before.

67

> The Lord said to him, "Surely I will be with you, and you shall defeat Midian as one man." So Gideon said to Him, "If now I have found favor in Your sight, then show me a sign that it is You who speak to me . . ." (Judg. 6:16-17)

The account of Gideon's role in history (Judg. 6-8) is most memorable for two things: for the colorful way God reduced the number of warriors Gideon would use to defeat the Midian oppressors; and for the number of tests Gideon used to verify that God was really the Author of the instructions he was getting.

It is easy to laugh at Gideon's hesitation, to be amazed at his presumption in asking for supernatural signs as proof that God was God. Was the man simply avoiding obedience? But it is important to note some things: that Gideon listened to God; that Gideon assumed it *might* be God speaking, and wanted to be sure; that God did not scold him for doing an identity check; and that Gideon eventually did exactly as he was instructed.

What if he had not responded as he did? What if Gideon had heard God's words, assumed it couldn't possibly be God, and never tried to check his assumption? Then that particular plan of the Father would not have been accomplished.

When God speaks to us, it is sometimes thrilling, but His primary purpose is not to thrill us but to accomplish His will. There are battles to fight, there are weary ones to encourage, there are crosses to be carried. We'll either catch His instructions or we won't. If we hear them, we'll either act on them or be stalled in uncertainty. If our hesitation is based either on scriptural principles or on the belief that we need further clarification, let us wait. But if we're mainly afraid that we'll look silly if it's just our own imaginations, let's ask God to purify our hearts so that we can step out in love and faith.

Because if it *wasn't* God speaking and we act on imagined directives, all we face is some inconvenience and humiliation. On the other hand, if it *was* God speaking and we don't obey, we will never know what glorious plan was never accomplished.

68

> Sacrifice and meal offering You have not desired; My ears you have opened . . . . I delight to do Your will, O my God; Your law is within my heart. (Ps. 40:6, 8)

Many people are uneasy about the idea of hearing the internal voice of God, or sensing the "nudging" of the Holy Spirit. What if it isn't the Lord, but just their own thoughts? Or what if it's actually the devil?

In this, we give ourselves little credit, and we give God none at all. Here is a story to illustrate what I mean. Years ago I picked up the phone, and a man's voice said, "Hi!" It sounded like my boyfriend Mike, who often called. "Hi, is this Mike?" I asked. "Yes, it's Mike," the man answered. I chatted for awhile about my doings, and the man gave friendly responses. But after a few minutes I began to realize that something didn't feel right, that it probably wasn't Mike on the phone at all. When I challenged the person about his identity, the truth became clear, and I hung up.

The call made me feel uneasy for awhile. But did I consider never answering the phone again? Of course not. We don't abandon our phone service because irritating telemarketers or truly unsavory people may try to engage us in conversations. We discern who it is and hang up if we need to.

Point one: Unsavory people will continue to use the same communications lines as our dear friends. Point two: We don't for any reason want to miss a call from a dear friend. Point three: A caller may fool us sometimes, but we will eventually figure it out.

God has opened our ears to hear His voice. If we don't hear it, we will miss a lot of what He wants us to do. He welcomes our carefulness: "Beloved, do not believe every spirit, but test the spirits to see whether they are from God" (1 John 4:1). The Counselor, the Holy Spirit, is always at hand to confirm what is from God and shed light on what isn't. But as the worship song says, we pray to "see Him more clearly, love Him more dearly, follow Him more nearly day by day." And we should have every expectation that He will be getting in touch.

> Your ears will hear a word behind you, "This is the way, walk in it," whenever you turn to the right or to the left. (Is. 30:21)

69

> Let those who love Him be like the rising of the sun in its might. (Judg. 5:31)

We humans have minds that can think in terms of numbers and organizational charts, intelligent allocations of money, resources, and personnel. The Bible reveals that this orderly thinking is in part a reflection of God's own nature. God had Moses number the people to organize the collecting of atonement money (Ex. 30). Later in history, God separated Gideon's army into two divisions, excused the larger one, and then repeated the process to get the personnel that would be adequate for the task (Judg. 7).

However, we and God may have different concepts about how many personnel and resources ought to be allocated for tasks or else placed in reserve. Gideon ended up defeating an army of many thousands with 300 men. Jesus fed 5000 people with five loaves and two fish and repeated the lesson on a second occasion. Furthermore, sometimes God may not want us to be concerned about our resources at all. David's frivolous census-taking of all the tribes of Israel ("that I may know the number of the people") was severely punished (2 Sam. 24).

Has the Lord shown you a formidable task He wants you to do? Love Him by acknowledging the strength that is with you, in you, and then moving forward in that strength. Believe God's words to Gideon (Judg. 6) as applied to the task He has set before you:

> The Lord is with you, O valiant warrior. Go in this your strength and do the task I've called you to do. Have I not sent you? Surely I will be with you, and you will accomplish it.

70

> As for me, I shall sing of Your strength; yes, I shall joyfully sing of Your lovingkindness in the morning, for You have been my stronghold and a refuge in the day of my distress. O my strength, I will sing praises to You; for God is my stronghold, the God who shows me lovingkindness. (Ps. 59:16-17)

The most powerful testimonies of God's mighty strength working in and through His children are those cases where the children are physically, functionally weak.

Moses begged God to reconsider His enormous plans for his life on the grounds that "I have never been eloquent . . . for I am slow of speech and slow of tongue." But God reminded him, "Who has made man's mouth? Or who makes him mute or deaf, or seeing or blind? Is it not I, the Lord?" (Ex. 4:10-11).

There is no physical infirmity through which God cannot pour His mighty strength and bring glory to Himself. We are rarely alone; God brings others alongside to help—Moses had Aaron, and later Joshua. And there is always His presence.

One modern-day testimony was Christopher Nolan, an Irish writer. Oxygen deprivation during a difficult birth left Nolan mute and quadriplegic. For a decade, he could only communicate with his family through eye movements. At age 11, a new drug relaxed his neck muscles, and Nolan began writing with a "unicorn stick" strapped to his forehead; he pecked a letter at a time on his typewriter as his mother held his chin with her hands. His prize-winning autobiography, *Under the Eye of the Clock*, was a glorious book full of prose that astounded the literary world.

"My mind is like a spin-dryer at full speed, my thoughts fly around my skull while beautiful words cascade down in my lap," he told *The Observer* of London in 1987.[7] The book also testified of the ever-giving love of a Christian family and community, and of a young man who knew his Maker. Describing his life in the third person, Nolan wrote, "Banished dreams always healed in the presence of God. In his Christian yearning for service, he bread-filled himself and his soul each time he received the sacred eucharist."[8]

No one would choose physical infirmity over youthful strength. But let's rejoice in God's amazing words to the apostle Paul on the subject (2 Cor. 12:9): "My grace is sufficient for you, for power is perfected in weakness."

71

But the Lord said to Samuel, "Do not look at his appearance or the height of his stature, for I have rejected him; for God sees not as man sees, for man looks at the outward appearance, but the Lord looks at the heart." (1 Sam. 16:7)

The righteous man will flourish like the palm tree, he will grow like a cedar in Lebanon. Planted in the house of the Lord, they will flourish in the courts of our God. They will still yield fruit in old age; they shall be full of sap and very green, to declare that the Lord is upright; He is my rock, and there is no unrighteousness in Him. (Ps. 92:12-15)

Though some cultures accord more respect to older people than others do, societies usually place their hopes on the young, the strong, and the beautiful. The young can be inspiring in their eagerness, energy, and fresh ideas. The strong give the appearance of reliability, of having what it takes to compete and win, and to bear the burdens of leadership. As for the physically beautiful, they have a personal charisma that seizes others' attention and says, "I'm an obvious candidate" when an important position needs to be filled.

Churches may overlook some of God's key players by seeing individuals as the world does, considering one person as too old, or too handicapped, or too unattractive to do certain tasks. As God's servants, we shouldn't covet positions of power, but rather make sure that we don't accept our value as defined by either the world or the church group we are part of, as a way of excusing ourselves from service. God has good works for us to "walk in," even if we reach the point where our legs give out on us.

72

> I shall run the way of Your commandments, for You will enlarge my heart. (Ps. 119:32)

> And Jesus answered, "You shall love the Lord your God with all your heart, and with all your soul, and with all your strength and with all your mind; and your neighbor as yourself . . . ." But wishing to justify himself, he said to Jesus, "And who is my neighbor?" (Luke 10:27, 29)

A wonderful evangelistic pamphlet called "The Four Spiritual Laws" begins by telling readers that God loves them and offers them a "wonderful plan for your life."[9] I would not deny the truth of that statement. Yet perhaps it's the wrong angle for conveying the biggest truth about Kingdom living. Because it suggests that the reader is at the center of a particular plan, is the key player. The truth is that any plan of God's will be more about God than about me; and it is likely to be less about me than about others and me, about *us*.

I would put it this way: God has wonderful *plans*, magnificent plans, plans for His servants to participate in, plans for those who don't yet know Jesus, plans for all creation. And my individual part is to know and love God well enough to get in on some of those plans.

What wonderful things is God doing? To use different word pictures, what plans is God sowing, growing, reaping? Could I join in?

How can I add a brick to His structures, or a talent or skill to assist in building one of them?

Is there already a wonderful river of service that I could be a part of? Is there a role, seemingly tiny, or big and obvious, where I could serve God by serving others?

And as I'm asking the Holy Spirit these questions, I am also letting God bring individuals into my awareness. How can I help this person along my path, someone trapped, or confused, someone literally or spiritually hungry, a person as clearly *my* neighbor as the injured man was suddenly a neighbor of the passersby in Jesus' parable of the Good Samaritan?

To the extent that I am willing to make Jesus the center, to love myself only as much as I'm learning to love others, I am someone that God can use in the unfathomable complexity of plans He has got going.

May God enlarge our hearts to the size He requires!

73

> Jesus presented another parable to them, saying, "The kingdom of heaven is like a mustard seed, which a man took and sowed in his field; and this is smaller than all other seeds, but when it is full grown, it is larger than the garden plants and becomes a tree, so that the birds of the air come and nest in its branches." (Matt. 13:31-32)

The other day I took a long pedestrian crossing at a downtown intersection. In the center was a wide traffic island, half of it sidewalk, the rest planted over. Rather than rush to get across before the light turned red, I decided to linger on the island and examine the foliage. I discovered it included quite a variety of small trees and bushes, several of them flowering, and no species had been repeated. Some large rocks were loosely arranged and could be sat upon. I reflected that someone had put a lot of thought into creating this tiny, pleasant oasis. Perhaps few pedestrians would make use of it; loud vehicles raced past it, sending out fumes. Yet those few who did linger for a moment could have their eyes refreshed by the small splashes of color, the variety of intricately-shaped leaves to be noticed, the restful arrangement of the scene.

In Jesus' parable about the mustard tree, the tree becomes a blessing to the larger world around it. It is like the tree in Psalm 1, "which yields its fruit in its season."

If we Christians can be seen as life-giving trees, offering the fruit of God's Spirit to all within reach, we are probably best positioned to serve people who are around us regularly: family members, fellow students, coworkers. But we can also love God by being alert and prepared to welcome the surprise visitors stopping by our garden. God may arrange an encounter around the edges of our life—on the traffic islands, so to speak.

Whether it is a stranger or a casual acquaintance, God has them pausing in our garden in need of a blessing.

74

> Then the King will say to those on His right, "Come, you who are blessed of My Father, inherit the kingdom prepared for you from the foundation of the world. For I was hungry, and you gave Me something to eat; I was thirsty, and you gave Me something to drink; I was a stranger, and you invited Me in; naked, and you clothed Me; I was sick, and you visited Me; I was in prison, and you came to Me . . . . Truly I say to you, to the extent that you did it to one of these brothers of Mine, even the least of them, you did it to Me." (Matt. 25:34-36, 40)

When Jesus said these words, He was speaking to an audience who knew that God cared very much for the destitute, for widows and orphans, for prisoners and slaves. God had instituted laws to get His people providing for the poor, and He had admonished them through the prophets when they followed religious observances but neglected people. "Is it a fast like this which I choose, a day for a man to humble himself? Is it . . . for spreading out sackcloth and ashes as a bed? . . . Is it not to divide your bread with the hungry and bring the homeless poor into your house; when you see the naked, to cover him; and not to hide yourself from your own flesh?" (Is. 58:5, 7)

When Jesus calls the hungry and sick "these brothers of Mine," He blesses His listeners then and now with a new understanding. These needy ones aren't just a problem for society to deal with, and they're not even just other human beings like ourselves—they are the King's brothers.

Many Christians are so far from grasping this implication in their souls that when they themselves suddenly face an economic crisis and slide down the scale from relatively rich to relatively poor, they feel great shame. They hate accepting help from others; they hate being identified with those in the world that they may have secretly despised.

We love the Lord when we embrace His perspective on the needy ones in our midst. Accepting the truth of their identity—"these brothers of Mine"—opens our minds and hearts to the particular commands God has for us. He is ready to show us how we're to serve them.

75

> He who has the seven Spirits of God, and the seven stars, says this: "... Wake up, and strengthen the things that remain, which were about to die; for I have not found your deeds completed in the sight of My God." (Rev. 3:1-2)

God sometimes uses tragedy in our lives as a wake-up call. For Bill Gates, the multibillionaire, it was the early death of his mother to cancer that caused him to decide that the time to begin serving others with his wealth was *now*, not ten or twenty years down the road; and the Gates Foundation was begun. God also uses other life experiences that extract us from our tidy routines and give us a hint of what His own eyes see. This happened to Scott Harrison, an American nightclub promoter whose firsthand encounter with poverty in Liberia transformed his world view 180 degrees. By his own account once extremely self-serving, Harrison became eager to serve the world's poor with the talents he had. Today his charity organization helps build wells in developing nations, providing clean water to millions.

In John's vision recorded in the book of Revelation, God tells the Sardis church that although they may appear alive, their way of functioning indicates that they are actually dead. These Christians have apparently been given much—"Remember, therefore, what you have received and heard"—but they are not using it to God's glory. They are like the "wicked, lazy slave" in Jesus' parable (Matt. 25) who did nothing with his fortune but bury it.

We love God when we respond to His wake-up calls in our lives with a willingness to let Him do a massive reorientation of our time, talents, and wealth. In love, we strengthen our obedience to His directions, as our time left on earth may indeed be short.

> Be ready; for the Son of Man is coming at an hour that you do not expect.... Who then is the faithful and sensible steward, whom his master will put in charge of his servants, to give them their rations at the proper time? Blessed is the slave whom his master finds so doing when he comes.... From everyone who has been given much, much will be required. (Luke 12:40, 42, 48)

76

> Listen carefully to Me, and eat what is good, and delight yourself in abundance.... For as the rain and snow come down from heaven, and do not return there without watering the earth and making it bear and sprout, and furnishing seed to the sower and bread to the eater, so will My word be which goes forth from My mouth.... (Is. 55:2, 10-11)

One way we love God with our minds is by listening carefully. When a father giving instructions to his child notices the youngster's eyes straying back to the toys he or she was playing with, he might say, "Honey, are listening? Look at me when I'm talking to you." The child has assumed the instructions aren't important, or that they are familiar ones (finish your homework, answer the phone for me) and therefore predictable.

The earthly father knows that his instructions *are* important, and possibly not the expected ones. As for our heavenly Father, His thoughts are often so high and unimaginable that without our full attention, they won't be caught by us at all.

When we *do* catch them, blessings abound in a chain reaction. This is because God's word is "seed to the sower and bread to the eater," and everyone gets to play multiple roles! When I listen carefully to God and catch His guidance, His teaching, His directions, I "eat" and am overcome with delight. When I share His lessons through my wise, loving speech and actions, others "eat what is good" as well. Later, they too may pass on "seeds" of that same word to yet more people. And with today's communication media, a spoken or written word could be caught by millions.

God's word is fruitful, life-giving. This seed is like a powerful anti-bomb, a bomb whose terrific explosion brings not death but widespread resurrection *life*. This seed is also like a missile which chases its target. "My word... will not return to Me empty, without accomplishing what I desire, and without succeeding in the matter for which I sent it" (Is. 55:11).

So let us listen hard and listen carefully. God's will is accomplished through our careful listening. After the Holy Spirit, we human servants are the primary sowers of God's word.

77

The fourth chapter of Daniel narrates the experience of Nebuchadnezzar, a king who learned the hard way where his strength came from.

Nebuchadnezzar has grown very proud, and Daniel interprets a vision God has given the king to warn him of the danger he is in. "You have become great and grown strong, and your majesty has become great and reached to the sky and your dominion to the end of the earth . . . . This is the decree of the Most High, which has come upon my lord the king; that you be driven away from mankind, and your dwelling place be with the beasts of the field . . . until you recognize that the Most High is the ruler over the realm of mankind, and bestows it on whomever He wishes . . . . Therefore, O King . . . break away now from your sins by doing righteousness, and from your iniquities by showing mercy to the poor, in case there may be a prolonging of your prosperity" (vv. 22-27).

Twelve months later King Nebuchadnezzar is enjoying a walk on his palace roof and reflects, "Is this not Babylon the great, which I myself have built as a royal residence by the might of my power and for the glory of my majesty?" (v. 30) Immediately God's word to the king is fulfilled, and he loses his mind.

"Love the Lord with all your strength." This narrative teaches us to remember first causes as we survey what our hard work, our brilliant strategies, perhaps our sacrificial efforts, have brought to a satisfying conclusion. Yes, we did it—but the strength to do all of it came from the Lord! Let us continually get our eyes off the accomplishments and back onto Him, in praise, thanksgiving, awe, humility. When others are impressed by what we have done, let us sincerely point them to the Author of our strength.

And when the achievements have brought power, wealth, influence, or leisure time, let us love God by using those assets as He directs, for His glory.

78

> The Father of mercies and God of all comfort . . . comforts us in all our affliction so that we will be able to comfort those who are in any affliction with the comfort with which we ourselves are comforted by God. (2 Cor. 1:3-4)

Our souls love rest. We read in Psalm 23 that "He makes me lie down in green pastures; He leads me beside quiet waters," and our souls respond with longing. We remember such times of peaceful restoration, and we look forward to more of them.

Yet this does not describe the normal Christian life, in which Jesus said we would have tribulation. While still on earth, we Christians must not expect to reach a permanent physical, emotional, material, and spiritual "comfort zone" where we will live happily ever after. Paul's letter above continues, " . . . if we are afflicted, it is for your comfort and salvation; or if we are comforted, it is for your comfort, which is effective in the patient enduring of the same sufferings . . ." (v. 6). When Paul wrote to the Corinthian Christians, God's love had already greatly expanded his heart and mind. His sufferings had stretched him. He had learned that there was nothing which could not be endured when Christ met him in the midst of it. By choosing faithfulness and clinging to God, Paul remained where God's love sustained him, comforted him—and built him up. When the suffering and heartbreak had passed, a stronger, more gifted servant remained.

God asks us, too, to accept the humbling, the losses, the disappointment, and the pain that He has chosen for us to bear. Our part is to love Him and refuse to let go of Him. Like Job, we declare our allegiance to our Father when the dust has settled: "The Lord gave and the Lord has taken away. Blessed be the name of the Lord." As we do this, over the days and weeks, each of us is built up in Christ into a servant who has more blessings to bestow on Christ's body—because we have suffered in ways that millions of others have, *and* have known God's consolation. It is not only that we have experienced the consolation and will forever have a powerful testimony to share, but that we ourselves are *full* of that consolation. Christ's love lives in us, and the Spirit leads us in the words and actions that bless others when their own times of suffering come.

79

> Go therefore and make disciples of all nations, baptizing them in the name of the Father and the Son and the Holy Spirit, teaching them to observe all that I commanded you. (Matt. 28:19-20)

> And He said to them, "Thus it is written, that the Christ would suffer and rise again from the dead the third day, and that repentance for forgiveness of sins would be proclaimed in His name to all the nations, beginning from Jerusalem." (Luke 24:46-47)

Jesus' final instructions to His disciples were to pass on the amazing good news that God had provided a way for every person, Jew or Gentile, to be reconciled with Him. In John's gospel, Jesus spells out to Peter that loving the Lord is synonymous with taking on the Lord's business as his own: in other words, loving those Jesus Himself loves and considering their lives and welfare to be top priority. "Do you love Me? . . . Tend My lambs . . . . Shepherd My sheep" (John 21:15-16).

Evangelism makes a lot of Christians very nervous. One year my city had a series of meetings featuring a famous evangelist, and local churches printed attractive invitation cards for their members to use in inviting friends and neighbors. I found myself uncomfortable about approaching certain colleagues whom I believed the Lord had brought to mind, and I began coming up with reasons that they probably wouldn't be interested anyway. Eventually the truth became clear: my reluctance was about *me*, not about *them*. I anticipated feeling embarrassed and awkward if they refused.

Loving Jesus means loving others enough that we are willing to give them the best chance possible to know the good news of salvation. When I grasped this truth, I could deliberately set aside my embarrassment, reject my fears, and seriously look for, pray for, and seize good opportunities to invite people.

Do we love Him? Then we must love *them*. They are sheep without a shepherd and He is the Good Shepherd. Loving Him means embracing His priorities as our own. And with the clarity of mind comes boldness in following through.

80

> Have I not commanded you? Be strong and courageous! Do not tremble or be dismayed, for the Lord your God is with you wherever you go. (Josh. 1:9)

Timidity does not accomplish the Lord's work. Boldness does. Boldness is a way of loving God with all our strength.

God has mercy and patience with the fearful. Yet He still calls them to obey His directives. Moses was terrified at the outset about the responsibilities God was laying on his shoulders. The prophet Elijah faithfully spoke God's words to powerful monarchs who hated him, until one day Elijah's faith crumbled and he ran for his life. In both of these instances, scripture records that God listened to His servants as they poured out their fears. He also corrected their perspectives, and encouraged them by promising helpmates for the awesome tasks ahead. Then He pointed them at the tasks He had prepared for them.

Timidity says, "I can't possibly." Boldness says, "I will go in the strength that You will give me."

"Be strong and courageous!" Boldness is a decision to acknowledge and take hold of the strength that God has already given us, and to move forward in faith; and to continue moving forward in the expectation that our faithful God will pour out more and more of His strength for the task at hand.

81

> Give me understanding, that I may observe Your law, and keep it with all my heart. Make me walk in the path of Your commandments, for I delight in it. (Ps. 119:34-35)

> All Scripture is inspired by God and profitable for teaching, for reproof, for correction, and for training in righteousness . . . . (2 Tim. 3:16)

I'm a city person, but I'm offering two stories about farm animals from first-hand experience. I'll call them "The Two Parables of the Goats." On a farm adjoining a university campus where I once taught, there was a very large, usually empty, pasture. In my wanderings there one afternoon, I came across two young goats. We were about the only creatures in the field that day, and I wondered if anyone was watching out for these two. Then I noticed a she-goat in the distance, whose head shot up at about the same moment I turned mine toward her. The mother goat let out a bleat, and the effect on her youngsters was instantaneous. They became anxious—possibly at the wide expanse separating them from Mom—and they immediately trotted homeward, bleating in response as they went.

In another country, years later, I lived in a small city surrounded by farms. The speed limit for vehicles was low within the city; as drivers left the city limit, the signs allowed them to practically double their speed. Then very soon a small bridge loomed up, eliminating visibility of the road beyond it, and signs directed vehicles to slow down to a crawl. Motorists usually obeyed the signs, and one day there was good cause to be glad we did. As I reached the top of the rise that day, I suddenly saw two goats calmly trotting side by side up the center of the opposite lane. No farmer was in sight in any direction, and these two were approaching an urban jungle. No doubt the drivers behind me, and those cautiously following the goats, had the same thoughts—I saw amusement, mixed with head shaking. These goats were headed for trouble which they had no notion of.

We live in a world which constantly tells us lies. It throws up idols for our worship. It preaches a value system directly at variance with the teachings of scripture, and it advocates a tolerance, even acceptance, of practices the Bible calls sin. When one hears lies repeated enough times, they can begin to sound plausible.

What's the solution? Perhaps the parables can suggest it. Stay close enough to the Lord that you hear His voice; you're always safe with Him. And stay off the world's paths. Read the Bible so that you know what it teaches—don't be content to take anyone else's word for it—and walk in the path of God's commandments.

82

> At the command of the Lord the sons of Israel would set out, and at the command of the Lord they would camp; as long as the cloud settled over the tabernacle, they remained camped.... Whether it was two days or a month or a year that the cloud lingered over the tabernacle, staying above it, the sons of Israel remained camped and did not set out; but when it was lifted, they did set out. (Num. 9:18, 22)

Throughout their forty years in the wilderness, the Israelites had daily experienced not only God's miraculous provision—the manna—but the miraculous evidence of His presence, the cloud over the tabernacle. "So it was continuously; the cloud would cover it by day, and the appearance of fire by night" (Num. 9:16). The cloud was over the Israelites as they traveled, and it remained over the tabernacle while they camped, waiting for it to move. The first time, they waited thirteen months.

The cloud was God's testimony to the people: "I am with you. The command is to stay camped." I wonder how often the people mused among themselves about the long wait to move forward to the new home God had promised them. Yet no matter how restless the people became, one sure thing prevented them from breaking camp and moving forward without permission: they had no idea where the "Promised Land" actually was. Only God could take them there.

The stationary cloud provided an ongoing exercise in humility. The people were obliged to be obedient to their new master, the God of love who had brought them out of slavery in Egypt, because they had no viable alternative. So they stayed put and they waited. Perhaps we Christians have an extra temptation to rebel today, when the Holy Spirit seems to be telling us to pause, to wait, to stop moving forward in a particular problem or project or relationship. Unlike the Israelites in the wilderness camp, we often think we know *exactly* where we need to get to. We resist the Spirit's counsel because it contradicts our sense of efficiency, or the plans that seem so sensible to us.

When it comes to honoring God, humility is a major theme in scripture, and presuming knowledge one doesn't have is sin. James writes, "Come now, you who say, 'Today or tomorrow we will go to such and such a city and spend a year there and engage in business and make a profit.' Yet you do not know what your life will be like tomorrow.... But as it is you boast in your ignorance; all such boasting is evil" (James 4: 13-16).

Let's take a tip from Moses, who, when asked to make a ruling on a point of law, recognized that only the lawgiver Himself could do that. Moses told the people, "Wait, and I will listen to what the Lord will command concerning you" (Num. 9:8).

83

When I remember You on my bed, I meditate on You in the night watches, for You have been my help, and in the shadow of Your wings I sing for joy. (Ps. 63:6-7)

And His name will be called Wonderful Counselor, Mighty God, Eternal Father, Prince of Peace. (Is. 9:6)

For the eleventh birthday of my godniece Ellie (she has both a godmother and a god-aunt), I wrote her a letter encouraging her ("now that you're eleven") to begin having her own devotional times. I explained that many Christians like to make time early in the morning to do this. Her response: "In your letter, you mentioned I might spend some time with Jesus. Actually, sometimes at night I just '*talk*' to him. Sometimes in my head, sometimes out loud."

Ellie's letter told me that the Holy Spirit was way ahead of me! He was already getting the child's attention, and at times of His own choosing. It is unlikely that Ellie's parents would have suggested post-bedtime night watches; in fact we adults don't usually expect God to call meetings with us "after hours." Yet He does. David writes, "I will bless the Lord who has counseled me; indeed my mind instructs me in the night" (Ps. 16:7).

The next line in that psalm is, "I have set the Lord continually before me." The more we seek to set the Lord continually before us, as Mighty God, Eternal Father, and Wonderful Counselor, the more we will hear Him in our minds; and the more we will notice that His conversational style is often unexpected. He'll call us to attention in the shower, on an escalator, at a traffic light—and sometimes in the middle of the night. How we respond is between us and God. Sometimes I have gotten out of bed to record an insight that I didn't want to commit to a sleepy memory. Sometimes I've sensed God wanting to show me a sin not dealt with, so I've gotten up to pray, lest I fall back to sleep. Whenever I wake up in the middle of the night now, I try to remember to check with the Lord who is continually before me: "Lord, any word? Or shall I go back to sleep?"

84

> Harlotry, wine, and new wine take away the understanding. My people consult their wooden idol, and their diviner's wand informs them; for a spirit of harlotry has led them astray, and they have played the harlot, departing from their God. They offer sacrifices on the tops of mountains and burn incense on the hills, under oak, poplar and terebinth, because their shade is pleasant. (Hos. 4:11-13)

Taiwan is a country in which many people serve a variety of gods, and an entire wall of the living room is often full of shelves, altars, pictures, and lamps dedicated to their worship. When someone becomes a Christian, the family of Christ gladly assists the new believer in carting off the paraphernalia. But some Christians are like my friend Mrs. Wang. The old idol furniture remains in the house because it is familiar to her and removing it still seems too radical a change. "After all," she reasons, "I'm not worshiping those false gods now, so it shouldn't matter if the stuff is still there."

For Christians in other cultures, Mrs. Wang's behavior may appear stubborn, or silly, or an indication that she hasn't really surrendered her whole heart to Jesus. But before we begin to feel spiritually superior to our Christian sister, let's let the Holy Spirit shine a light in our own living rooms.

What magazines sit on the shelves? Are we spending our free time meditating on the latest exploits of movie idols? Glancing at "our" star signs in astrology columns ("just for a laugh!")? Lusting after photographs in other magazines hidden out of sight? What books are we reading? Are the hours spent vicariously living in their stories, or letting the authors speak to us, moving us *closer* to truth or *away* from it? And then there are the television and the computer. What TV programs usurp the attention of everyone in the living room on a weekly basis, where people's minds may be just as receptive as they are in the church pew on Sundays? What cyberworlds are we secretly visiting from our computer portals, "because their shade is pleasant"?

We serve a loving and forgiving God. But our sins can eventually cause havoc in our lives. We may become like those described in Hosea's prophecy: "Their deeds will not allow them to return to their God. For a spirit of harlotry is within them, and they do not know the Lord" (Hos. 5:4).

We want to love God with all of our hearts and minds. Let's not wonder what foolishness God will let us get away with. Instead, let's ask Him to bring all of our deeds into the light and show us how to deal with our particular home furniture.

85

> Now when the attendant of the man of God had risen early and gone out, behold, an army with horses and chariots was circling the city. And his servant said to him, "Alas, my master! What shall we do?" So he answered, "Do not fear, for those who are with us are more than those who are with them." (2 Kin. 6:15-16)

Further on in this exciting passage of scripture, Elisha's fearful servant is miraculously permitted to see God's own powerful army of angels in formation around the two of them.

The scripture doesn't tell us whether Elisha's own eyes ever viewed the army, or whether his awareness of it came from the Holy Spirit. But we see here two ways of responding to danger on the horizon, and many Christians can identify with both responses.

Elisha's response is calmness and confidence. He deeply believes the truths written in the Psalms: "Through God we will do valiantly, and it is He who shall tread down our adversaries" (108:13); "You who fear the Lord, trust in the Lord; He is their help and their shield" (115:11). Elisha knows the history recorded in the scriptures, battles where God leads His army to win victories when the Israelites are outnumbered, even battles where He performs miracles that overpower the enemy in advance of any military action.

Many Christians can remember times that they too have lived in the promise in Isaiah 30:15, "In quietness and trust is your strength." Yet we also sympathize with the servant's response of terror. The enemy included "horses and chariots and a great army," enough to terrify anyone, and we're glad God allowed the servant to see the mightier heavenly army as well. But there is an important lesson for us here: the servant panicked because he didn't see the whole situation from God's perspective. When our minds focus on a horror that we see before our eyes, we too can be overwhelmed by fear.

God's servants are called to pray continuously in a spiritual battle which is ongoing, and to never be paralyzed by fear. "Resist the devil and he will flee from you. Draw near to God and He will draw near to you" (James 4:7-8). We love God with our minds when we reject the temptation to dramatize a terrifying situation, either to ourselves or to others. We must turn our minds from the terror and look on God.

86

> Exalt the Lord our God, and worship at His footstool—He is holy. Moses and Aaron were among His priests, and Samuel was among those who called upon His name; they called upon the Lord, and He answered them. (Ps. 99:5-6)

> He has made us to be a kingdom, priests to His God and Father. (Rev. 1:6)

We have many roles to play in our lives, and it is good to pause sometimes to see if we are fulfilling our duties adequately. How am I doing as a parent, as a spouse, as an employee, as a supervisor, as a team member, as a friend and neighbor? Stopping to reassess these relationships once in a while can help us to adjust our time and energies; perhaps we're spread too thin, or perhaps we've been avoiding tough problems.

By using roles we are familiar with, our God helps us to understand the nature of the relationship which He, a spiritual being, desires to have with us humans. We are sheep of a Shepherd; servants of a Master; children of a Father; and we are priests to our God. As we seek to love God with all that is within us, we can meditate on these roles; we can stretch our minds toward God and ask Him to teach us how to fulfill the accompanying duties in our own lives.

"Shepherd, am I following You faithfully in this situation? Master, tell me what You want here, and I'll obey. Father, I'm hurt, scared, lonely, so I've come to You." The priest's primary function is to minister to God—to perform acts of praise and worship to the King of Kings. His second major function is to intercede between God and other people, to pray to God in their behalf.

Love God by embracing the role of priest and letting Him teach you how to fulfill it.

> You also, as living stones, are being built up as a spiritual house for a holy priesthood, to offer up spiritual sacrifices acceptable to God through Jesus Christ. (1 Pet. 2:5)

87

> It is I [God] who answer and look after you. I am like a luxuriant cypress; from Me comes your fruit. Whoever is wise, let him understand these things; whoever is discerning, let him know them. (Hos. 14:8-9)

> You shall follow the Lord your God and fear Him; and you shall keep His commandments, listen to His voice, serve Him, and cling to Him. (Deut. 13:4)

The spirit of tithing in scripture is that it is the first fruits, the tenth immediately taken off the top as automatically belonging to the Lord. Many Christians find the practice simple, even satisfying, when it comes to giving money to the church. Once the habit is established, it isn't hard to continue with it.

Much more challenging to persevere with are the "tithes" of our time. God introduced this principle with the Sabbath days and the various festivals where His people drew apart to rest and eat and worship. As committed disciples, we know that the regular practice of quality-time dates with God is basic to our relationship with Him. We are loving Him when we set aside the blocks of time and protect them from encroachments; when we come to Him with rested, undistracted minds; when we don't rush in with our own concerns but wait for Him to set the agenda.

How easy it is sometimes to not deliberately choose God *Himself,* and instead choose pleasant pastimes that seem to promise some of the "flavor" of God: a wonderful Christian book or movie, for example. We may happily spend hours engrossed in it, telling ourselves it's a sort of private time with God. Yet we usually find that it's not. Even if we digest lessons from the book or film that the Lord will use in our lives, we have not been sitting at Jesus' feet. Instead, we've been sitting with our own feet up, indulging in what one writer calls "an emotional cream puff," a vicarious experience of others' dramas. Like the Israelites in the wilderness who grew weary of the daily diet of manna and rebelled, we decided to change the menu . . . and found that nothing, nothing is a substitute for feasting on Jesus' presence.

Entertainment which meets the standards of Philippians 4:8 is a blessing to partake of. It is true and honorable, pure and praiseworthy, and an excellent way of spending our leisure time . . . which does not happen to include the time we have set aside to offer our Lord. We love and honor Him by keeping our commitments.

88

> Consider it all joy, my brethren, when you encounter various trials, knowing that the testimony of your faith produces endurance. And let endurance have its perfect result, so that you may be perfect and complete, lacking in nothing. (James 1:2-4)

> We also exult in our tribulations, knowing that tribulation brings about perseverance; and perseverance, proven character; and proven character, hope; and hope does not disappoint, because the love of God has been poured out within our hearts through the Holy Spirit who was given to us. (Rom. 5:3-5)

Some who read the above verses will nod and think to themselves, "Yes, I know." While serving in yoke with Jesus, these Christians have learned that it is possible to go through monotonous periods of fixed routine, endless setbacks, even "the valley of the shadow of death," and endure. And not only endure the situation but persevere in the midst of it to love God and listen for His commands. Other Christians, those who have had fairly soft lives so far, may realize that they themselves are novices when it comes to perseverance.

Perseverance is not a virtue which is modeled a lot in modern life. We pursue speed and efficiency in manufacturing, food preparation, and communication. (The perseverance of the scientific pioneers and inventors happens behind closed doors.) Perseverance takes time, so it is hard to portray its essence in films because of their time constraints. Books describe it better, and long accounts of the details of persevering in a task can be both fascinating and exhausting to read. The narratives allow us to feel something of what it means to hold fast through tedium, through difficulties, through danger and pain—hold fast because of the worthiness of the goal.

We need to learn perseverance, do perseverance. The book of Revelation mentions it a lot. Christians need it when times get tough, and the scriptures promise that times are going to get much tougher. We want Jesus to be able to say of us what He says of the church at Ephesus in John's vision, "You have perseverance and have endured for My name's sake and have not grown weary" (Rev. 2:3).

89

The book of Nehemiah is the account of how God used one faithful man to lead the huge undertaking of rebuilding the wall around Jerusalem, which lay in ruins. The city itself was desolated, and it was surrounded by enemies who immediately recognized the future danger of having a fortified Jerusalem in their midst. Nehemiah's account is a powerful illustration of the battle we Christians must wage against our enemies in the spiritual realm. Here are a few sections, in Nehemiah's words.

> Our enemies said, "[The builders] will not know or see until we come among them, kill them and put a stop to the work." (4:11)

> I stationed the people in families with their swords, spears, and bows. When I saw their fear, I rose and spoke to the nobles, the officials, and the rest of the people: "Do not be afraid of them; remember the Lord who is great and awesome, and fight for your brothers, your sons, your daughters, your wives and your houses." (4:13-14)

> Half of my servants carried on the work while half of them held the spears the shields, the bows and the breastplates . . . . Those who were rebuilding the wall and those who carried burdens took their load with one hand doing the work and the other holding a weapon . . . . Neither I, my brothers, my servants, nor the men of the guard who followed me, none of us removed our clothes, each took his weapon even to the water. (4:16-17, 23)

Our battle against Christ's enemies is as real as the battle in the book of Nehemiah. Peter gives a frightening, tangible picture of just how real our adversary is. "Be of sober spirit, be on the alert. Your adversary, the devil, prowls about like a roaring lion, seeking someone to devour" (1 Pet. 5:8).

We love God by offering up our strength for the battle; by following our Captain's instructions in using that strength; and by remembering that Satan doesn't call time out while we take a water break.

90

> Rejoice always; pray without ceasing; in everything give thanks; for this is God's will for you in Christ Jesus. (1 Thess. 5:16-18)

When we want to please God, this piece of scripture can look daunting. The prospect of always needing to rejoice can seem so impossible—even unfair—that we may not try to consider the other two big commands in the verse. Yet if we did manage to pray continually and to thank God in every circumstance, we probably wouldn't need to be commanded to rejoice. Love, joy, peace, and all the rest would be flooding out of us.

It is important to balance Paul's teaching in his letter to the Thessalonians with what he writes to the Romans: "Rejoice with those who rejoice, and weep with those who weep" (Rom. 12:15). Yes, it is possible to rejoice in times of tragedy, but only when we are rejoicing in truths that are greater than the present horrible circumstances.

What does God teach us that we can rejoice about, and thus give love and honor to Him?

1. *That God is righteous and just.* "Your right hand is full of righteousness. Let Mount Zion be glad, let the daughters of Judah rejoice because of Your judgments." (Ps. 48:10-11)
2. *That God is in control.* "The Lord reigns, let the earth rejoice; let the many islands be glad." (Ps. 97:1)
3. *That God has saved us.* "My heart shall rejoice in Your salvation. I will sing to the Lord, because He has dealt bountifully with me."(Ps. 13:5-6)
4. *That we are forever His.* "Rejoice that your names are recorded in heaven."(Luke 10:20)
5. *That God can be trusted.* "Our soul waits for the Lord; He is our help and our shield. For our heart rejoices in Him, because we trust in His holy name." (Ps. 33:20-21)
6. *That God is continuing to bring others into His kingdom.* "Rejoice with me, for I have found my sheep which was lost!" (Luke 15:6)

Rejoicing in these things is one way of setting our minds on the things above, of loving God with all our minds.

91

> In repentance and rest you will be saved, in quietness and trust is your strength. (Is. 30:15)

When we are looking for scriptural models of people that God was pleased with, scripture itself has three candidates: Noah, Daniel, and Job. Four times in Ezekiel 14, God states that if these men were in a sinful nation which God intended to punish, they would not be able to save the nation, but "they would deliver (only) themselves by their righteousness."

The book of Daniel shows us a man of powerful faith, great determination and discipline in prayer, and complete loyalty to God. Along the way, the narrative also shows a man who became physically and emotionally spent in the course of his labors for God and took the correct action.

Daniel had undertaken an extended period of prayer and partial fasting, and after three weeks he received a terrifying vision from God. The experience exhausted him. "No strength was left in me, for my natural color turned to a deathly pallor." Daniel fell into a deep sleep, and when he awakened, the angel in the vision told him that he was about to receive "an understanding of what will happen to your people in the latter days" (Dan. 10:8-14).

Daniel was still speechless, overcome. When he was finally enabled to speak, he acknowledged his need:

> "O my lord, as a result of the vision anguish has come upon me, and I have retained no strength. For how can such a servant of my lord talk to such as my lord? As for me, there remains just now no strength in me, nor has any breath been left in me." Then this one with human appearance touched me again and strengthened me. He said, "O man of high esteem, do not be afraid. Peace be with you; take courage and be courageous!" Now as soon as he spoke to me, I received strength, and said, "May my lord speak, for you have strengthened me" (Dan. 10:16-19).

The cooperation of Daniel and God illustrates the relationship between strength and rest, the balance between "I can do all things through Christ who strengthens me" and "He gives to His beloved sleep" (Phil. 4:13, Ps. 127:2). Daniel devotes his strength to serious prayer, and its climax depletes his strength. God grants him deep sleep. Daniel pleads that he still lacks strength. God does something else to strengthen him. Daniel acknowledges that he has been strengthened, and he tells God he is now ready for service.

Here is a model for loving God with all our strength.

92

"Remember the sabbath day, to keep it holy." (Ex. 20:8)

Many Christians aren't quite sure what to think about the sabbath day (also spelled Sabbath Day) commandment, the fourth of the Big Ten. Jesus said that He did not come to abolish the Law or the Prophets (Matt. 5:17), but He himself did miraculous healings on the sabbath and taught His followers not to be legalistic about refraining from all work on this day of rest. Another thing that seems to relegate the commandment to ancient history is that after Jesus' resurrection on a Sunday, Christians gradually established Sundays (not Saturdays) as their special day for assembling together.

Is the sabbath commandment an important one? We want to love the Lord. What does He require of us?

Moses emphasized to the Israelites that the commands were given *for* them, for their good (Deut. 10:13). Jesus also emphasized that the sabbath was made *for* people. And the scriptures contain an awesome promise for those who honor the day of rest:

> If because of the sabbath, you turn your foot from doing your own pleasure on My holy day, and call the sabbath a delight, a holy day of the Lord honorable, and honor it, desisting from your own ways, from seeking your own pleasure and speaking your own word, then you will take delight in the Lord, and I will make you ride the heights of the earth . . . (Is. 58:13-14).

Love God by acknowledging this commandment as given for your good and open up your life, your days, to Him. Ask God how He wants you to obey this command, whether it will be Saturday, or Sunday, or some other time block that will be set aside in order for you to desist from your own ways and simply take delight in Him.

A modern-day testimony may serve as an encouragement. In an interview for *Discipleship Journal*, Eugene Peterson, author of *The Message*, was asked what spiritual practice had most shaped his walk with God. His answer: "Keeping a weekly sabbath." Peterson said it was a day that he and his wife set aside to "lay and pray." "No other decision has made so much difference to our lives across the board. It has impacted our marriage, children, church life, friendships, writing . . . the works."[10]

93

> He has told you, O man, what is good; and what does the Lord require of you but to do justice, to love kindness, and to walk humbly with your God? (Mic. 6:8)

In my experience, doing kind things and just things can seem like a piece of cake compared to walking humbly with God. The reason is that my pride sometimes gets me pushing my own agendas to accomplish justice, and jerking people around in my efforts to be kind and helpful. A part of me wants to make all the decisions about running the show, and also somehow be the one to carry everything out. Moreover, I want everything to be perfect, and of course it never is.

My gracious God is teaching me what it means to have a humble heart, the only sort of heart He is willing to have deep communion with. The lessons below may help others who struggle with egos that get in their way.

Lesson #1: There are some things I cannot do easily, some I don't do well. With others' help, encouragement, ideas, or training, I may be able to do the things better. Or maybe I'll always do them just adequately.

Lesson #2: With some tasks, I need to rejoice that someone else can, and will, do them instead of me.

Lesson #3: With some tasks, I may need to accept that "adequate" is exactly what is needed. "Excellent" may mean something showy but unnecessary, surplus that will be wasted and could have been used elsewhere.

Lesson #4: All tasks, all things, I am to do unto the Lord. I'm to do them with the time, talent, and strength He gives me. I'm not to try to do them *perfectly*; I'm not to become my own audience, applauding what seems excellent, kicking myself for making a mistake. Instead, I'm to keep my mind clear about the purposes of the task, and look up occasionally from my planning or executing to wait on the Lord. "Lord, will this (tool, task, project, meeting, phone call, action, rearrangement) serve Your purposes? Or should it be something different? Something more? Something less?"

As Gideon discovered, it may indeed be something less.

94

> Turn to my reproof, behold I will pour out my spirit on you;
> I will make my words known to you. (Prov. 1:23)

> He whose ear listens to the life-giving reproof will dwell among the wise. (Prov. 15:31)

Reproof is censure, official disapproval of something we have done. It isn't a word we hear or read often, partly because they aren't many who have the authority to reprove us: parents and teachers if we've misbehaved; judges if we've broken the law; and God when we've sinned.

Reading the above verses may make us a bit uneasy. How could a person have anything but negative feelings toward a rebuke, a scolding? Much as we might welcome God's spirit poured out on us, the idea of turning to His reproof sounds a bit like walking into a tidal wave.

Yet God's reproofs are always given in love, thrown out as lifelines to haul us back to safe waters before our sins truly cause us to sink. We love Him by listening well. And the actual experience of recognizing His voice of reproof can be awesome.

Some years ago I was in a women's fellowship group which began with a time of praying together. Shortly before we got started, I had a conversation with a member who sometimes played the piano for us. She was saying how uncomfortable she felt playing now that she'd found out I played more skillfully. I proceeded to give this friend a lecture on how we are all God's tools, to be used in the ways He chooses; that the tools are never perfect ones, but only need to be good enough. (I was rather pleased with my grasp of these truths and how well I was expressing them.)

A few minutes later we gathered for prayer, and the person leading us that day followed our usual format: once the praying began, individuals spoke aloud in turn, sometimes with long-winded prayers, often repeating what had already been prayed for. Afterwards, as we repositioned the chairs for Bible study, I began complaining to myself (as I often did) about the prayer format, and wondering why the wonderful Christian leading us today hadn't followed my previous advice and led us in a more effective prayer method. And suddenly I had my first experience of hearing the voice of God inside my mind. It was powerful, and rich with irony: "Isn't the tool good enough?" It was my own "lecture" flung back in my face.

Such reproof was overwhelming, and I was silent for the next hour. What overwhelmed me most was that God spoke to me personally to correct my understanding. His was "life-giving reproof," to help me "dwell among the wise."

95

In the case of two of the three men God singled out to call righteous (Ezek. 14), scripture records another similarity between them. Both men practiced intercession, lifting up prayer for the sinful hearts of others, begging for God's compassion and forgiveness.

> When the days of feasting had completed their cycle, Job would send and consecrate [his sons], rising up early in the morning and offering burnt offerings according to the number of them all; for Job said, "Perhaps my sons have sinned and cursed God in their hearts." Thus Job did continually. (Job 1:5)

> I [Daniel] gave my attention to the Lord God to seek Him by prayer and supplications, with fasting, sackcloth, and ashes. And I prayed to the Lord my God and confessed and said, "Alas, O Lord . . . we have sinned, committed iniquity, acted wickedly, and rebelled, even turning aside from Your commandments and ordinances . . . . Open shame belongs to us, O Lord, to our kings, our princes, and our fathers, because we have sinned against You." (Dan. 9:3-5, 8)

When we love God with all our hearts, we move beyond "me" prayers to prayers for others God shows us. Job prayed faithfully for his children, "rising up early in the morning." Daniel devoted days and weeks to prayer for the scattered Jewish nation. He identified himself with his much more sinful countrymen: "*we* have sinned, committed iniquity." Job and Daniel stood in the gap between God and others, building a wall of prayer.

> First of all, then, I urge that entreaties and prayers, petitions and thanksgivings, be made on behalf of all men, for kings and all who are in authority . . . . This is good and acceptable in the sight of God our Savior, who desires all men to be saved and come to a knowledge of the truth. (1 Tim. 2:1-4)

96

> Finally, be strong in the Lord and in the strength of His might.
> Put on the full armor of God, so that you will be able to stand
> firm against the schemes of the devil. (Eph. 6:10-11)

In churches, the "Lord's supper" (or "communion") and water baptism are taken seriously. It is understood that there is a spiritual nature to the physical ritual. Thus, we determine not to be too distracted by the trivial details of collecting the small cups afterwards, or the awkward way in which the baptismal gowns cling when wet. We want to cooperate with God's mysterious ways by accepting His means.

Many Christians aren't sure how to take Ephesians 6:10-18, which describes each piece of the armor of God. The writer does use some figurative language earlier in the letter as a way to illustrate spiritual mysteries; God's people are described as a building with Jesus as cornerstone, and then they are described as a body with Jesus as head. However, if the instructions about putting on or taking up the six pieces of armor seem to be metaphoric, the other instructions are certainly not. We are commanded to be strong in God and His mighty power because it's an unimaginably powerful enemy that we are facing. We are told to pray with every variety of prayer there is, "on every occasion," and to be particularly faithful about praying for other Christians.

We believers bow our heads (or kneel, or lift our hands up) to pray because it helps our minds when our postures echo the attitudes we seek: reverence, honor, expectation. If we accept the words about the armor as having a literal application, then speaking about and even acting out the instructions may have effects we can only imagine. It will certainly help us to get our minds around some deep spiritual truths.

One might simply pray, "God, by Your strength, I take up the full armor You've prepared." Another person might pray this and then name each piece. I myself—where no one would see me and grin—act out the process of donning the armor, as I tell God and the heavenly realm that I am putting on the helmet of salvation, and so on. With each piece, I usually add words that declare more about that armor. "The Lord is my righteousness. I stand in His righteousness, not my own."

Love God with all your strength—and put on your armor, so you'll be able to stand against the devil and wield that sword of the Spirit.

97

> Flee immorality. Every other sin that a man commits is outside the body, but the immoral man sins against his own body. Or do you not know that your body is a temple of the Holy Spirit who is in you, whom you have from God, and that you are not your own? For you have been bought with a price: therefore glorify God in your body. (1 Cor. 6:18-20)

The Bible talks a lot about the sin of sexual immorality. Jesus says it is one of the things which come out of the heart and defiles us (Matt. 15:18-20). It makes us filthy; it contaminates us so that our hearts are no longer pure; it corrupts our souls. Sexually immoral persons are also listed with the murderers and sorcerers whose "part will be the lake that burns with fire and brimstone" (Rev. 21:8).

Sexual sin is not addressed very much in some churches today except in classes for the church youth. Pastors probably consider the Bible's teachings on the subject to be well-known to all; they may also hesitate to deal with such a messy topic in a Sunday church service. Yet Christians who desire to love and obey God need both to understand the powerful nature of this sin and to take practical steps to stay out of it.

In 1 Corinthians 6:15-20, Paul explains why sexual sin is particularly lethal. On a spiritual plane that our minds can only accept by faith, our bodies are "members of Christ." When a Christian joins his or her body with another person, "The two will become one flesh." Yes, this is what happens in a marriage relationship—God intended for it to happen there. But with immorality, the body has been defiled—it has been deeply joined with the wrong person, not just physically but spiritually. This has serious repercussions.

Christians who fall can repent and be restored. The scriptures encourage getting others involved in the repentance process. "Confess your sins to one another, and pray for one another, so that you may be healed" (James 5:16). As for those of us who by God's grace are on the straight path, or restored to it once again, let's pray for the wisdom to recognize the ways and means that Satan uses in our individual lives to tempt us into sexual sin. We must expect that there *will* be temptations, for few adults are immune. And at the first sight of one, we must exit the situation, for the love of God.

> The highway of the upright is to depart from evil; he who watches his way preserves his life. (Prov. 16:17)

98

> The Lord saw that the wickedness of man was great on the earth, and that every intent of the thoughts of his heart was only evil continually . . . . Noah was a righteous man, blameless in his time; Noah walked with God. (Gen. 6:5, 9)

One of God's "righteous men" played a role in one of the Bible's most dramatic narratives—the building of the ark and the Great Flood. Noah modeled obedience to very clear but unusual commands, and in the weeks spent building his large boat miles from the sea, his neighbors probably questioned his sanity.

The colorful events that generations have named "Noah's ark" were almost the only part of Noah's long life that got recorded. Yet the lines of scripture above give us a clue about his earlier years. Noah lived in an age in which no one on earth was seeking God. No one was choosing righteous ways over evil ones, was walking with God instead of hiding from Him like Adam and Eve had—no one except Noah himself.

Surely this fact is just as extraordinary as the events surrounding the ark. With no more genetic inclination toward good than his countrymen, and with absolutely no encouragement from his society toward righteous living, "Noah was a righteous man, blameless in his time; Noah walked with God." Building the ark was one-time obedience, possibly much easier than the years of consistent obedience that preceded it. Noah made daily choices to bear the derision of society and walk to the beat of an entirely different drummer, his Creator and Lord.

Noah's life is a lesson not only that a person can be "blameless in his time," but that one's "time" is no excuse at all for sin. When the whole world is pursuing this, or being entertained by that, or participating in this, or paying tribute to that, we Christians are always called to walk with our God, to avoid every appearance of evil. The Evil One may tell us that to live God's way is too extreme, that certain compromises are necessary to stay current, to be accepted, to be "palatable" so that people won't be put off by Christianity.

Let us, like Noah, daily choose to love God and walk with Him. It's the life we were created for.

99

> My soul cleaves to the dust, revive me according to Your word.... My soul weeps because of grief; strengthen me according to Your word. (Ps. 119:25, 28)

What do we do when someone hurts us badly? Or when something happens which is so devastating that there seems to be no one to blame unless it's God? What do we do with emotional pain that hits us like a body blow?

So often our response to pain is to "solve" it: to treat pain as a problem which needs to be either gotten rid of or run from. We may turn to drink, do drugs, overeat, or try other excessive behaviors to bury the pain, hoping it will work its way out of our system. Or we may flee from the situation where the pain broadsided us—we may resolve to leave the job, or the church, or the family, or the friendship where we were suddenly hit so hard. If there is no exit available to us, perhaps we secretly roll up our souls so they resemble armadillos, and we determine not to let ourselves be hurt in the same way again.

Over a dozen times in Psalm 119, the writer testifies that when he is in anguish, he turns to God by reading the scriptures. "Revive me according to Your word.... Behold, I long for your precepts; revive me through Your righteousness.... Revive me according to Your lovingkindness.... Sustain me according to Your word, that I may live; and do not let me be ashamed of my hope.... Revive me according to your ordinances" (vv. 25, 40, 88, 116, 149). He also testifies that God answers such prayers: "This is my comfort in my affliction, that Your word has revived me" (v. 50).

When little children are hurt, they know to run home. There they hopefully receive comfort, medical aid, and sometimes good advice for handling future blows. We love and honor our heavenly Father when we run first to Him with our pain. And even when our souls are too troubled to hear God's voice in prayer, we can open the scriptures and ask our Father to read them to us.

> Make Your face shine upon Your servant, and teach me Your statutes. (Ps. 119:135)

100

> I will walk within my house in the integrity of my heart. I will set no worthless thing before my eyes; I hate the work of those who fall away; it shall not fasten its grip on me. (Ps. 101:2-3)

> O send out Your light and Your truth, let them lead me; let them bring me to Your holy hill, to Your dwelling places. Then I will go to the altar of God, to God my exceeding joy; and upon the lyre I shall praise You, O God, my God. (Ps. 43:3-4)

In David's day, even a king's house was limited in the number of "worthless things" he could set before his eyes. Perhaps David was thinking of sensuous dancing performances that would entice him to lust, or of items considered "lucky" because they invoked the favor of false gods. Whatever he had in mind, he was aware that what he set before his eyes had the potential of fastening its grip on his heart and eventually causing him to drift away from the intimate relationship he had with his Lord.

Attempting to put specific names to "worthless things" in today's world moves the Christian into a dangerous area. Is a pastime (or book or movie or computer activity) worthless because it wastes my time without renewing me in any way? Or is it worthless only if I overdo it, or if it leads me into sinful attitudes such as lust, coveting, or greed? And what if a fellow Christian claims that the thing which has such a powerful negative impact on me has no effect on him or her at all?

Our goal is to love the Lord with all our minds and hearts, letting His light and truth lead us closer and closer to Him. We are not called to judge our brothers and sisters but to obey the directives God is giving us. And they won't be the same for everyone. My friend Anne is clear that God asked her to give up fantasy novels. I myself have to avoid certain types of films because of the way my brain replays the images months and years afterwards. My short, buxom friend Michelle understands that perusing magazines with gorgeous, over-slim models leads her into thoughts of discontent. For another friend, the Internet itself has become a potentially worthless thing because of the constant temptation to check email and to spend minutes or hours reading the latest news on the celebrities of the moment.

> Turn away my eyes from looking at vanity, and revive me in Your ways. (Ps. 119:37)

101

> As you have received Christ Jesus the Lord, so walk in Him, having been firmly rooted and now being built up in your faith, just as you were instructed, and overflowing with gratitude. (Col. 2:6-7)

> . . . always giving thanks to God the Father for everything, in the name of our Lord Jesus Christ. (Eph. 5:20 NIV)

For years I lived on the fourth or fifth floors of walk-up apartments, glad for the low rents in these older buildings. My last was a three-bedroom place in a nice, safe neighborhood with a wonderful neighbor.

Then a serious knee problem dictated the end of my youthful days of racing up and down stairways. On my doctor's advice, and with the wonderful provision of God through friends' contacts and assistance, I moved to a bright new studio apartment in a high-rise where my rent was actually lower than before.

How grateful I was for mold-free cabinets and working faucets, for the beautiful parquet floors! For the first time ever, I had a view of the hills beyond the city, and I was content. For a time. And then I began to mourn. I missed the possessions I'd given away because there was no place to store or display them; I missed having lots of space to exercise or simply stroll around in.

Fortunately, for many years I had had a hero to remember whenever I felt sad about the loss of conveniences in my life, about the loss of physical abilities through accident or aging. My hero was Joni Eareckson Tada, the Christian paraplegic who has so blessed others with her books, talks, and the *Joni and Friends* ministries. When my earlier operation on a painful bunion was only partially successful, I could remind myself, "But you can walk!" When the current knee problem ended years of joyful hiking, I could be thankful that I'd had so many years already, and that the last hike was a glorious one with special friends.

As I sighed over my tiny studio apartment, it was downright embarrassing to recall what Paul wrote (Phil. 4:11-12) of being content in all circumstances, whether having abundance or suffering need. By no stretch of the imagination was I suffering! So I turned my wistful longing for past pleasure to thankfulness for present provision. And God has given me more reasons to be thankful. It takes 90 minutes to thoroughly clean my apartment; I now live so near cheap, healthy eating places that I need never cook. And these benefits are freeing up more hours so that I can write this book.

102

Glory in his holy name; let the hearts of those who seek the Lord rejoice. Look to the Lord and his strength; seek his face always. (Ps. 105:3-4 NIV)

Rejoice in the Lord always. Again I will say, rejoice! Let your gentleness be known to all men. The Lord is at hand. (Phil. 4:4-5)

Sometimes these beautiful verses of scripture seem to resound in our hearts as we read them, and our souls affirm, "Yes, Lord, yes!" Yet other times we read them and feel confronted: "I'm feeling anything but joyful today—does that mean I'm sinning? Am I supposed to try to drum up some positive emotions in myself? Or pretend to be joyful until I actually am? Or at least pretend to be joyful so that I don't become a burden to those around me?"

As we move forward in learning to love God with more of our hearts and minds, we need to remember that while God is the begetter of that love—we love because He first loved us—His own love is of a higher quality. His love is infinite in strength and unchanging. *Our* love is subject to our human weaknesses, so it wobbles; it's tossed about on our physical and emotional tides; it gets tainted with distractions.

Jesus says that if we obey the foremost commandment, and its corollary of loving others, we are doing what God requires. The verses above describe one aspect of loving God closely and well: we will be rejoicing in Him. But the rejoicing is a part of the whole. It is both a continuing effect and a continuing cause of continually seeking the Lord and His strength. It is bound up completely with "seeking His face always."

Scripture is, as Paul writes, profitable for correction. On days that we read such verses and they don't resound in our souls, even in a quiet way, we should ask the Holy Spirit to search our hearts to see if there is a hidden attitude that needs to come into the light. If there is, He will show us. Or perhaps He will show us that we need more sleep.

And when our hearts do rejoice in the Lord of life, what others will see is not necessarily a bubbly person covered in smiles. They will see a gentle spirit. And it is this gentle spirit which will testify to all people that the Lord is very near.

103

> God . . . reconciled us to himself through Christ and gave us the ministry of reconciliation: that God was reconciling the world to himself in Christ, not counting men's sins against them. And he has committed to us the message of reconciliation. We are therefore ambassadors, as though God were making his appeal through us. (2 Cor. 5:18-20 NIV)

In the apartment complex where I live, a guard sits in a small cubicle at the gate. One day after I had passed through with a smile and the usual "Good morning," I felt the Holy Spirit impressing on me to go back and tell the man that God loved him. I haven't done much on-the-spot evangelism with virtual strangers, so the conversation was short. "Do you know that God loves you very much?" "Uh, yes, of course," he answered, "God loves everyone." "Oh, good, you know that," I said, and on I went to catch my bus. Morning greetings were a bit stiff for a while after that. Then one morning the guard was wearing an eye patch, and I stopped to find out the reason; he had poked himself with the stem of his glasses. Though I am not usually an empathetic person, I nevertheless found myself really feeling for the man, and I broke into a short prayer aloud that God would quickly heal him, in Jesus name. The next day he didn't have the eye patch, and yes, the eye was better. "Oh," I said, "then we need to thank God, because He's our healer. Thank You, God!"

I have a job—three different part-time jobs, in fact. But I'm learning that one way I love God is by accepting the "job" He has given me as a reconciler. The other evening as I stepped out of a store, I had to slow down a bit for an old man in front of me. Suddenly tears came to my eyes as I thought of my own father, dead over a decade, who may not have had a relationship with God. And then the Holy Spirit reminded me that this man, too, was someone's father, someone's husband, someone's son, someone's dear friend—and he, too, needed Christ. I never saw the man's face, but I prayed for him in the minutes that followed.

In the letter to the church at Corinth, Paul writes, "We always carry around in our body the death of Jesus, so that the life of Jesus may also be revealed in our body" (2 Cor. 4:10 NIV). This identification with Jesus is crucial. It keeps us seeing others with Jesus' eyes. It keeps the windows of our minds open to opportunities to connect with the dear ones God wants to reconcile to Himself. We are His representatives, His ambassadors, saying, "Come, come into God's kingdom!" and praying, "May they come!"

104

> Give heed to me and answer me. I am restless in my complaint and am surely distracted because of the voice of the enemy, because of the pressure of the wicked . . . . My heart is in anguish . . . . Fear and trembling come upon me, and horror has overwhelmed me . . . . As for me, I shall call upon God, and the Lord will save me. Evening and morning and at noon, I will complain and murmur, and He will hear my voice. He will redeem my soul in peace from the battle which is against me. (Ps. 55:2-5, 16-17)

Many Christian writers have pointed out that the mind is a spiritual battleground. And indeed most of the battles, both small ones and the ones we later recall as major turning points in our lives, are events that take place when we're by ourselves. They are often times when we're looking back on recent happenings, replaying things people have said; we're reacting to situations that threaten us, rejecting false insinuations; fear and anger are swarming around our heads like angry hornets.

The writer of the psalm above had this experience, and the worst horror was that the enemy was originally "my companion and my familiar friend." Betrayal and treachery are the kind of sins which can crush our souls and hurl them into prison, because we are filled with a desire to strike back. In fact, it is possible that the writer was still in his mental prison, because he begged God to bring down his former friend "to the pit of destruction."

But David, the writer, knew the way out of his anger and anguish. "I shall call upon God, and the Lord will save me . . . He will redeem my soul in peace from the battle which is against me." And this is our way out as well. We love God by crying out in those times when our mind is distracted with distress, oppressed by real and imagined scenarios—crying out to *Him*, not to friends who will take our part, not to the world at large. We cry out to God and admit our fears, our anger, and our pain.

Let God bind your wounds and strengthen you.

> Cast your burden upon the Lord and He will sustain you; He will never allow the righteous to be shaken. (Ps. 55:22)

105

> Behold, God is my helper; the Lord is the sustainer of my soul. (Ps. 54:4)

Between David's youth as a shepherd and the time he actually reigned as king, he spent years on the run from Saul. Part of that time, he and his followers lived in nearby Gath under that king's protection, acting as soldiers when Gath needed their services. 1 Samuel 29-30 records a bleak time in David's life when several terrible events happened one after another. As a result of slander, David was unjustly forced to leave Gath with his men and their families at a day's notice; three days later, their new home city was burned by raiders, who also kidnapped all of the women and children; and David's men were so bitter that they spoke of stoning him.

No one could blame those men for being bitter. We wouldn't be surprised to learn that David became bitter too, bitter against a God who hadn't fulfilled His promises, or that he collapsed under the strain. Yet he didn't do either. Scripture records, "But David strengthened himself in the Lord his God" (1 Sam. 30:6).

God's strength is always there, always sufficient. When we have been battered by a disaster, or a series of them, we can choose to lie in the dust; or we can choose life. We can use the last bit of the strength God has already given us to reach out in faith toward Him for more of that strength.

> I love You, O Lord, my strength. The Lord is my rock and my fortress and my deliverer, my God, my rock, in whom I take refuge; my shield and the horn of my salvation, my stronghold. (Ps. 18:1-2)

> Choose life . . . by loving the Lord your God, by obeying His voice, and by holding fast to Him; for this is your life and the length of your days. (Deut. 30:19-20)

106

> I took them out of the land of Egypt and brought them into the wilderness. I gave them My statutes and informed them of My ordinances, by which, if a man observes them, he will live. Also I gave them My sabbaths to be a sign between Me and them, that they might know that I am the Lord who sanctifies them. (Ezek. 20:10-12)

Throughout the world, Christians whose job description is "fulltime ministry" fall into the habit of using their assigned rest day (often Monday, the day after a busy Sunday) to continue taking calls, planning programs, and doing other church work. They reason that this is God's work, and therefore it must take precedence over rest.

One Christian leader has written of a time when illness removed him from active ministry for some months. "During my period of illness I really struggled. I didn't really want to rest in God alone. Instead, I wanted to rest in the *work* of God. I realized again that I was a laborer who worked without real peace from the Lord. I loved *doing* things for the Lord so much that it had become my security and my source of joy. God wanted to remove this idol from my life."[11]

When we find ourselves resisting true breaks from our regular work, the times of rest allotted to us by our employers, times that we could well use to simply "take delight in the Lord," we should examine our hearts. We might ask:

Am I assuming that I know more than God? Am I ignoring a scriptural principle because I believe it doesn't apply to me? (Exodus 31:17 says, "On the seventh day He [God] ceased from labor, and was refreshed.")

Do I believe that the particular work God has given me cannot be done without my total involvement all day, seven days a week? Do I not trust that God's six-day plan is the right one?

Has my work, including my work "for God," become more important to me than God Himself? Have I forgotten that part of my service of worship is to sit at Jesus' feet, as Mary did, and simply listen?

By skipping times of rest and renewal, have I let small sins slip into my life that I'm not dealing with? Am I losing my godly perspective on sin?

Trusting and obeying God's commandments brings great blessings. With the sabbath commandment, one blessing is that we get to continually watch for God's miraculous provision. We get to watch *Him* accomplish more in six days than we could ever accomplish in seven.

107

> Who will separate us from the love of Christ? Will tribulation, or distress, or persecution, or famine, or nakedness, or peril, or sword? Just as it is written, "For Your sake we are being put to death all day long; we were considered as sheep to be slaughtered." But in all things we overwhelmingly conquer through Him who loved us. (Rom. 8:35-37)

Christians who are privileged to live in a country which is not experiencing food shortages, war, or religious persecution may shudder as they read the above and hope that they never have to test the truth of these words of scripture. Yet millions of other Christians, past and present, have proved their truth for themselves and often for others as well.

Some years ago, three missionaries were kidnapped and held for ransom. The women knew that their captors' demands would not be met. The mission organization had no funds for enriching criminals; also, paying off the kidnappers would put other missionaries at risk. Before their deaths, the women managed to send out a message to those who would understand: "Habakkuk 3:17-19." ("Though the fig tree should not blossom and there be no fruit on the vines, though the yield of the olive should fail and the fields produce no food, though the flock should be cut off from the fold and there be no cattle in the stalls, yet I will exult in the Lord, I will rejoice in the God of my salvation. The Lord is my strength, and He has made my feet like hinds' feet, and makes me walk on my high places.")

If missionaries might expect to face a fierce trial, a certain kindly stay-at-home man did not, a man known for being "blameless, upright, fearing God and turning away from evil." Yet Job had his possessions, his children, and his health torn from him in a day. He had never expected to have to overcome such devastation of his life, made worse by the criticisms of his friends; but he did. "It is still my consolation, and I rejoice in unsparing pain, that I have not denied the words of the Holy One" (Job 6:10).

We love God when we determine to build ourselves up on our most holy faith so that when tough times come, we are ready to be conquerors, for His glory.

> God is our refuge and strength, a very present help in trouble. Therefore we will not fear, though the earth should change and though the mountains slip into the heart of the sea . . . . (Ps. 46:1-2)

108

> I am the Alpha and the Omega, the beginning and the end. I will give to the one who thirsts from the spring of the water of life without cost. He who overcomes shall inherit these things, and I will be his God and he will be My son. But for the cowardly and unbelieving and abominable and murderers and immoral persons and sorcerers and idolaters and all liars, their part will be in the lake that burns with fire and brimstone, which is the second death. (Rev. 21:6-8)

Jesus clearly taught that it is our attitudes as much as our actions that display our sin before God, no matter how nice we may seem to other people. We understand that lustful fantasies and hateful attitudes toward others put us in the categories of immoral persons and murderers, and we confess such sins. The surprise in the scripture passage above is the category at the head of the list: the cowardly.

How could cowardice be sinful, we wonder. Doesn't being afraid and turning and running just *happen*, so that it's not really a person's fault? In fact, most nations throughout history have judged that cowardice is indeed a person's fault, and soldiers who desert in time of war are usually executed.

Being brave in the day of battle means determining to stand, not run, because God is the Commander in Chief and we want to honor and obey Him with all that is within us. He has given us the strength to make this determination—we love Him by exercising that strength to the utmost. In faith, we call out to God and we tap the vast resources of God's mighty strength, "the surpassing greatness of His power toward us who believe" (Eph. 1:19).

> On the day I called, You answered me; You made me bold with strength in my soul. (Ps. 138:3)

109

> With all prayer and petition pray at all times in the Spirit, and with this in view, be on the alert with all perseverance and petition for all the saints. (Eph. 6:18)

Imagine an ancient warrior outfitted with the best armor available, whose mind was so occupied with his own thoughts that he missed seeing signs of the enemy's approach. Or imagine a modern soldier, equipped for heavy action, but unable to hear the officer's instructions because he is listening to the popular music he's got blasting into his earphones.

Those who refer to the armor of God in Ephesians 6 often say that it is really *seven* pieces, not six. The belt of truth, the breastplate of righteousness, the shoes of the gospel of peace, the shield of faith, the helmet of salvation, the sword of the Spirit—and prayer. Not just token prayer, but *all* prayer and petition at *all* times with *all* perseverance and for *all* the saints. (The Greek equivalent for "all" does appear four times in the original passage.)

This is a strong command for Christians. Pray at all times? Does God want us to become prayer machines? No, but He does need prayer warriors. He needs those who are determined to keep their minds alert—not obsessively tuned in to their own mental scenarios. The warriors have learned to pray in the Spirit "and into it staying awake with all constancy," as one Greek translation renders it.[12] Because they are deliberately alert, the warriors notice when the Spirit brings to mind a friend or family member or church leader or missionary. They respond by not just idly thinking about the individuals but speaking to God about them, asking for God's mercy and favor and wisdom and protection in their lives.

"At all times" sounds daunting in English; the Greek can be rendered "in all seasons," the sense being that there is no activity that need keep us from praying in the Spirit. Ask God what this would mean in your own life.

110

> "Simon, Simon, behold, Satan has demanded permission to sift you like wheat; but I have prayed for you, that your faith may not fail; and you, when once you have turned again, strengthen your brothers." (Luke 22:31-32)

Halfway through the writing of this devotional, I responded to a call at church for volunteers to help with preparations for a holiday party for some special guests. I was keen to help; but as a teacher and writer who is not used to taking direction, I knew I would need to prepare my mind if I was to be a help and not a hindrance. So I prayed for a willing, humble heart, and God answered my prayers. Besides the expected task of wrapping presents, there were unexpected ones like pumping air into balloons that had a tendency to burst in our faces; but God's peace reigned in my heart. With the abundance of ready hands, the work was finished early, and we sat down in little groups to rest and wait for the guests to arrive. And within fifteen minutes, in my group of acquaintances, I had begun to be opinionated, dictatorial, and critical toward someone in the group, toward people in general, and toward one of our church's programs. Eventually I began listening to myself, stopped talking, and decided that I wouldn't stay for the party.

As I headed home, I asked the Holy Spirit to show me my sins, and I repented. The breastplate of Jesus' righteousness was protecting my heart; thus, I didn't indulge in accusations against myself for falling short of godliness. But in a part of my mind I still sighed. How could someone like me write a devotional?

When I awoke the next morning, God spoke the answer to my question. The answer was that I was Peter, not Jesus. Peter (Simon Peter) was the disciple who piped up to offer his own suggestion at the miraculous transfiguration event (Matt. 17) and was interrupted by the voice of God admonishing him to listen to His Son. Peter was the one who boasted that he would die for Christ rather than deny Him, and then did the opposite three times. Peter was the one who wasn't content to hear his own mission from Jesus but wanted to know John's mission as well.

Let's thank God that the scriptures about Jesus' ministry are so full of this very flawed disciple. Jesus was Peter's Lord, and the book of Acts tells us of the wonderful ways God used the man. As we too strive to love our Lord with all that is within us, He will use us as well. But when we fail—and sometimes we will—let's not be thrown by our failure, and let's never, ever, lose our faith in Him.

111

> Those whom I love, I reprove and discipline; be zealous, therefore and repent. Behold, I stand at the door and knock; if anyone hears my voice and opens the door, I will come in to him . . . . (Rev. 3:19-20)

Verse 20 above is often used in evangelism, to give those who don't know Jesus a mental picture of Him knocking on the door of their hearts. It is a powerful metaphor, but in fact it was originally said to a church full of Christians, the church at Laodicea. These Christians felt they must be doing fine because their lives were going smoothly in terms of their financial needs. ("I am rich, and have become wealthy, and have need of nothing" [Rev. 3:17].) Perhaps they subconsciously felt that their comfortable lifestyle was even proof that God was pleased with them, that their successful investments were a reward for good behavior.

Or if they were wise enough to avoid that trap, they may have fallen into another one. As they amassed more and more wealth, perhaps they experienced a sense of relief. Surely those days of not knowing where next week's meal was coming from were gone forever? Perhaps they began to take a tremendous amount of comfort and security from their wealth. "Give us this day our daily bread" no longer had the urgency it once did. Without realizing it, these Christians may have allowed their minds to become clouded, and to feel that financial independence, economic security, was the real goal of their lives. And so they lost their zealous love for Jesus, their eagerness to take His directions. They lost God's perspective on things. Jesus told them, "You do not know that you are miserable and poor and blind and naked" (Rev. 3:17).

The angel in John's vision recorded in Revelation said that the messages for the seven churches were meant for all Christians. He said seven times, "He who has an ear, let him hear what the Spirit says to the churches." We love God by giving attention to the messages, and, as we read, listening for Jesus' voice at the door of our own hearts.

112

> Jesus said to His disciples, "If anyone wishes to come after Me, he must deny himself, and take up his cross and follow Me. For whoever wishes to save his own life will lose it; but whoever loses his life for My sake will find it. For what will it profit a man if he gains the whole world and forfeits his soul?" (Matt. 16:24-26)

The above passage is very familiar to most Christians, and it makes some of them a little uneasy. They think of St. Francis of Assisi, and of the rich man whom Jesus told to give away all he owned (Mark 10); and they resist the idea that God would ask them to make any radical changes in the current arrangement of their lives. They reason that surely God has blessed them with their job and their house (and perhaps a long list of other possessions, not to mention good schools for the children). They hesitate to ask the Lord if they are personally obeying His commands to "Follow Me" and "Lose your life for My sake."

I believe that following Jesus means being willing not only to die as a martyr if necessary, but to let go our tight grasp on the lives we've set up for ourselves. When it is *my* life, I might see it as something like this.

my importance	my preferences	my entertainment	my feelings
my family	my best friends	my other friends	my enemies
my meals	my home	**ME** / my job	my laundry
my God		my success	my priorities
	my role in the church	my tithes and offerings	
	my influence	my hopes and plans	

The "my's" go on forever. They fill my mind.

If I determine to follow Jesus fully, to love Him enough to let go of all the "my's," I become one of a myriad of precious servants, all greatly loved by Jesus the King. And we are all living in a world full of others whom Jesus wants to bring to Himself. I am available to pray for, telephone, work alongside, rejoice with, mourn with, and wash the dirty feet of anyone Jesus wants me to. The more I love Jesus, the more He fills me with love for my fellow servants, near and far, and He connects me with them in deeper and more surprising ways. "My job" becomes "the place where I am salt and light, the place where God has plans for me to bless others with my talents, my love, and my availability to serve as He directs." It's not my life anymore; it's His. And I can trust Him that there will be food on the table, and the laundry will get done.

113

Feeling neglected and forgotten by a very close friend, I began what became a series of painful, angry emails volleyed back and forth between us. Just at the point when all I wanted was to back off and consign the friendship to the dust, I had two dreams.

The first night I dreamed I was babysitting an infant for friends, and through my neglect it almost died. The second night there was another dream about a baby. This time I was with detectives trying to work out when it had died, and it turned out to be an earlier time of death than I had assumed, and I was somehow involved.

As I awoke the morning after the second dream, I asked God if there was a message for me in these nightmares. He gently showed me that the baby was the vital friendship I was managing to choke the life out of with my recent proceedings.

> Indeed God speaks once, or twice, yet no one notices it. In a dream, a vision of the night, when sound sleep falls on men, while they slumber in their beds, then He opens the ears of men, and seals their instruction, that He may turn aside man from his conduct, and keep man from pride. (Job 33:14-17)

Not every dream is a message from God, just as not every shade tree that withers contains the serious lesson God intended one tree to have for Jonah. ("You had compassion on the plant for which you did not work.... Should I not have compassion on Nineveh, the great city in which there are more than 120,000 persons...?" [Jon. 4:10-11].)

But God seeks us out far more often than we do Him. If we sense the Lord may be trying to get our attention, we show Him love and honor by asking Him if that is the case.

114

> "But you, when you pray, go into your inner room, close your door and pray to your Father who is in secret, and your Father who sees what is done in secret will reward you." (Matt. 6:6)

> "But you, when you fast, anoint your head and wash your face so that your fasting will not be noticed by men, but by your Father who is in secret; and your Father who sees what is done in secret will reward you." (Matt. 6:17-18)

The prophet Isaiah says of God, "You meet him who rejoices in doing righteousness, who remembers You in Your ways" (Is. 64:5). What a promise! When the greatest desire of our hearts is to do righteousness, to do the things that will please God, He will meet us in our times of prayer and in our actions.

"You meet him who rejoices in doing righteousness." We love God by seeking those private meetings with Him, those times of secret closeness which are no one else's business. He meets us as we set aside blocks of time for prayer and fasting so that we can be with Him to worship Him, honor Him, listen to Him. He meets us as we respond to the Spirit's directive to give to someone in need, perhaps more than we believe we can afford. Wouldn't others be impressed! But Jesus warns us that this loving response to God's call must be kept a secret. "Beware of practicing your righteousness before men to be noticed by them; otherwise you have no reward with your Father who is in heaven" (Matt. 6:1).

> Make me know your ways, O Lord; teach me Your paths.
> (Ps. 25:4)

115

> Do nothing from selfishness or empty conceit, but with humility of mind let each of you regard one another as more important than himself; do not merely look out for your own personal interests, but also for the interests of others. (Phil. 2:3-4)

My Taiwanese colleague and I were closing up the building one evening when she heard me whistling a tune. "Oh, don't whistle," she said seriously. "It will bring ghosts." A linguistic pun popped into my mind—foreigners were once derogatively referred to as "Western ghosts" in the Chinese language. So I quickly retorted with a grin, "The whistling has already brought one—a Western ghost!"

On the way home later, the Holy Spirit replayed the interchange for me, this brief dialog with a coworker, a rare time when she and I weren't talking about work. And now I understood some things I had missed at the time: my colleague had been truly shocked by my light-hearted whistling, and she wanted to warn me before I invited unfriendly spirits onto the premises to hurt us all. She was bound by fear, whereas I had the knowledge that could specifically address that fear—Jesus could set her free.

We love Jesus when we keep a rein on our tongues, being "quick to hear and slow to speak" and not just when we're angry. Depending on our personalities, we may be inclined to make cute remarks, or vent frustration, or leap to defend ourselves, or idly say the first thing that pops into our minds. But when we hold back momentarily in order to really listen to what others are saying, trying to understand their thought processes, reaching to God for a response that will bring light and peace to the situation—that's love. It's agreeing with the truth which our human nature constantly clamors to contradict: God has each of us in a particular setting with particular people primarily so that we can bless them, not so that we can express ourselves and fill the air with our own thoughts.

Loving God with our minds includes deliberately reflecting on the eternal aspects of very mundane-looking circumstances. For my colleague, for my neighbor, for my relative, for the grocer, banker, sales clerk, bus driver, and stranger God brushes me up against, I am potentially a God-link. I am *their* God-link. These many dear ones are precious in God's sight. May the words that we are "slow to speak" be ones that bless.

116

> "Do not store up for yourselves treasures on earth, where moth and rust destroy, and where thieves break in and steal.... But store up for yourselves treasures in heaven... for where your treasure is, there your heart will be also.... No man can serve two masters; for either he will hate the one and love the other, or he will be devoted to the one and despise the other. You cannot serve God and wealth." (Matt. 6:19-21, 24)

Some of Jesus' clearest teachings are about how His followers are to treat money. Much as we may wish we could pursue both worldly wealth and spiritual wealth with equal fervor, Jesus says it's not possible. Why? Because if we serve God with love and devotion, and He suddenly calls us to open our hands wide to the poor, we may have to utterly reject the plans we had for increasing our wealth.

Furthermore, when we believe the Holy Spirit is directing us to give, we had better think twice about consulting others' opinions on the prompting. Jesus teaches, "Do not let your left hand know what your right hand is doing, so that your giving will be in secret" (Matt. 6:3-4). I believe that besides keeping our giving a secret from others, Jesus' metaphor about the two hands includes not reflecting too much on this God-directed giving ourselves, whether before, during, or afterward. I am not to use one hand to pat myself on the back with approval, or use it to point to my action as a marvelous gesture for a Christian to make; God knows what I've done, and I know, but even *I* should detach myself from contemplating the subject as soon as I can.

God deals with His servants individually, and in the end it is His approval alone that matters. When He speaks to our hearts about passing on a portion of the wealth He has provided, let's obey with the joy that King David's subjects showed in supporting the construction of the temple. "The people rejoiced because they had offered so willingly, for they made their offering to the Lord with a whole heart" (1 Chr. 29:9).

David rejoiced too, and we can echo his prayer:

> "O Lord our God, all this abundance that we have provided to build You a house for Your holy name, it is from Your hand, and all is Yours.... [So] with joy I have seen Your people,

who are present here, make their offerings willingly to You. O Lord, the God of Abraham, Isaac, and Israel, our fathers, preserve this forever in the intentions of the heart of Your people, and direct their heart to You" (1 Chr. 29:16-18).

117

> For though we walk in the flesh, we do not war according to the flesh. For the weapons of our warfare are not carnal but mighty in God for pulling down strongholds, casting down arguments and every high thing that exalts itself against the knowledge of God, bringing every thought into captivity to the obedience of Christ. (2 Cor.10:3-5)

As wise citizens of God's kingdom, we do well to remember that the main way the Holy Spirit speaks to us is through our minds. We hear Him best when our minds aren't jammed with competing thoughts. One of the benefits of going into a closet to pray, as Jesus instructed His followers to do, is that it eliminates visual distractions that get our thoughts wandering off in other directions. (Closing one's eyes to pray, whether in a church service or at home, can also help to shut out temptations to consider a friend's new dress or the dusty condition of the furniture.)

But solitude reveals to us that our minds are often very busy. When the sound of the TV and the pictures on the computer screen have been turned off, we become aware that the mind is a stage of its own, with lots of action on it. We find images and ideas that reflect the day's input of films, books, and conversations; we find attitudes about situations and people; and when we seek God, we become aware of the Holy Spirit shining His light on it all.

We love God with our minds by agreeing to cast down all thoughts, images, and attitudes that do not honor Him. We cast down judgment of others. ("Here's what Sam *ought* to do, so why doesn't he?") We cast down setting up the future as if we were gods. ("Here's exactly what I'm going to tell her if I have the chance.")

We don't let our thoughts capture us; instead we love God by capturing our rebellious thoughts and making them obey Christ. For example, I see a fellow Christian sinning and find myself thinking smugly, "Yes, there he goes again." I capture that thought by confessing my lack of love, and by thanking God that He loves my brother and can bring him to repentance for the sin; and I ask God to move in my brother's behalf.

118

> All of them were trying to frighten us, thinking, "They will become discouraged with the work and it will not be done." But now, O God, strengthen my hands. (Neh. 6:9)

While writing this book, I had a nine-day Lunar New Year holiday along with the rest of the country, and I expected to devote much of it to working on this book. Some work was done, and some enjoyable times with friends took place. But overall, I fell into my typical unhealthy vacation pattern of too much casual eating, too little exercise, and novel-reading to the point of eye strain. Instead of spending more time communing with God, I spent less; and instead of dealing with my own unwillingness to apply the discipline of a light schedule, I focused on the cold, rainy weather as the reason for my mild malaise.

But God used the reading stint to good purpose, because one paperback I picked up was *Close to the Wind*, an autobiographical account of some long-distance solo sailing done by Pete Goss. Much of the book describes Goss's necessarily unvarying routines for keeping his boat a strong, working vessel, and his environment a healthy place to live for months at a time. Sometimes there were storms at sea, and long repair jobs had to be done under exhausting, life-threatening conditions. And after a storm, no matter how fatigued he was, Goss disciplined himself to do the regular clean-up and maintenance jobs that would keep him and his boat functioning well.

The evidence of Goss's strength of mind and perseverance amazed me, until I remembered that he had spent nine years in Britain's Royal Marines. Those years were a perfect training ground for working toward his goal of sailing around the world single-handed.

We Christians need perseverance to daily accept the yoke and walk with Jesus and do the works that have been prepared for us to do. Like Nehemiah, we know that our strength for taking up the burden will come from God. Our part is to then continue walking in that strength,

> strengthened with all power, according to His glorious might, for the attaining of all steadfastness and patience; joyously giving thanks to the Father, who has qualified us to share in the inheritance of the saints in Light (Col. 1:11-12).

119

> Jotham became mighty because he ordered his ways before the Lord his God. (2 Chr. 27:6)

Some people are born into cultures, or families, which emphasize the importance of diligence, the disciplined pursuit of goals. In parts of Asia, for example, children spend years in hard preparation for university entrance tests. Then there are individuals who may not have this background, but have minds that love order; thus they are able to make long-range goals and follow through on them.

When it comes to perseverance, these people have a head-start. At the opposite extreme are those who grow up in societies that emphasize independence, variety, free choice. They are likely to resist setting routines for themselves, seeing it as "regimentation." As Christians, these people may find it hard to step daily under the yoke with Christ.

But we all need to remember that this is a yoke which we chose. We chose life, to love and obey God. Nothing in the scriptural histories of those who have gone before us indicates that this choice makes life smooth and comfortable. We will need perseverance to live the life God calls us to live.

How will we acquire perseverance? Essentially the same way that Pete Goss did—by practicing it. By persevering in the activities we know we should do and getting better and better at controlling the mind's resistance and complaints.

We can practice perseverance by faithfully doing the daily tasks which we know will bless God, bless ourselves, and bless those to whom we are responsible. We do appropriate cleaning, tidying, and food preparation tasks. We maintain habits of regular exercise, wise eating, and sufficient sleep. We perform our jobs and family duties, looking for opportunities to encourage and cooperate with others. Most important of all, we are faithful to our "dates" with God. When events disrupt our regular schedule, we can pray for wisdom about shortening or skipping certain tasks, perhaps on an alternating basis.

But we must strive to give time with God first place, first priority. We need His counsel, His strength, His grace. Once again, the main thing to remember is to keep the main thing the main thing.

120

> Because of the multitude of oppressions they cry out; they cry for help because of the arm of the mighty. But no one says, "Where is God my Maker, who gives songs in the night, who teaches us more than the beasts of the earth and makes us wiser than the birds of the heavens?" (Job 35:9-11)

Many people have come to faith during wartime, when they cried out to God in desperate fear, sometimes making rash vows about their futures "if You only save my life." A term has developed to describe them: foxhole Christians. When peace comes, many foxhole Christians keep their promises to God, but others do not. They acknowledge that God was faithful while they themselves were not; but faithfulness seemed a boring pursuit, and the pleasant pastimes of peace much more colorful and inviting.

Scripture teaches us that God went through this process of broken promises with His chosen people time and time again. He saved them from their oppressors, and before long they forgot Him, disobeyed Him, and wandered after other gods. He sent prophets to warn them, and when they didn't listen He sent oppressors to make them desperate enough and humble enough to seek God once more.

What is it about the simple pleasures of the world that claim us so easily? It is probably the fact that they *are* pleasures—restful fun, sometimes exercising our bodies and/or our minds in ways that are energizing and satisfying as well. So we may divide our lives into two compartments: the things we *have* to do (jobs, everyday tasks related to running a home and raising kids, church meetings we put on our schedule) and the time we have left for . . . simple pleasures.

The scripture above reminds us that God Himself is in the business of providing simple pleasures. If we unplug ourselves from our portable music, we may discover that He, too, has songs for us, both old and new. News programs and Internet sites can feed our minds with data and opinions in an interesting, easily palatable format. But let's remember that the Author of wisdom has things to teach us as well. As we look at passages of the Bible, certainly; but also as we simply spend "down time" with Him, puttering comfortably around the house, letting the Holy Spirit join our reflections on what we're doing, reading, noticing. Love the Lord by opening your down time to Him with all your heart.

121

> In Him was life, and the life was the Light of men . . . . This is the judgment, that the Light has come into the world, and men loved darkness rather than the Light, for their deeds were evil. For everyone who does evil hates the Light, and does not come to the Light for fear that his deeds will be exposed. But he who practices the truth comes to the Light, so that his deeds may be manifested as having been wrought in God. (John 1:4, 3:19-21)

Little children are filled with curiosity about the world, and their fearless exploration can move them into dangerous situations when their elders aren't nearby. Their fascination with their own and others' bodies, for example, typically leads to some games of Doctor/Patient—innocent games, yet games which might get out of hand, because they tend to be played in private places, away from the adults.

    A friend of mine remembers that he and his childhood playmates liked to play such secret games outside under the family's big country house. His parents were wise; whenever things got too quiet under there, they would simply call, "Hey, kids, come on out where we can see you." And out the kids would come, back into the sunshine, back where those who loved them could protect them from harm. Any tendencies their games might have had toward evil quickly disappeared in the light.

    We love our heavenly Father by keeping ourselves "out where He can see us." When we find ourselves burrowing deeply into a form of solitary entertainment—an online game, a novel, any pastime that may engage us for hours at a time—we are wise to pray David's prayer:

> Search me, O God, and know my heart; try me and know my anxious thoughts; and see if there be any hurtful way in me, and lead me in the everlasting way (Psalm 139:23-24).

122

"He who loves his life loses it, and he who hates his life in this world will keep it to life eternal. If anyone serves Me, he must follow Me; and where I am, there will My servant be also . . . ." (John 12:25-26)

When I read these verses, I have a mental picture of a mountain trail where Jesus is a bit out in front, looking back to see if I'm following, and then moving around the next turn of the trail. And I'm eagerly keeping up, because I'm determined not to miss a thing.

Life on earth is short. Days are short. We simply cannot do all the delightful or important or meaningful things we might do if we had 48-hour days and lived to be 150. There is a limit to careers one can pursue; languages, musical instruments, technical skills one can master; people one can spend regular time with; countries one can explore; recreational activities one can find time for in a month. When a person is fairly young, fairly healthy, and not burdened with poverty, there is often an urge to see and do as much as possible, to taste all the richness that life has to offer.

But again, our time is short. The author of Ephesians writes, "Be careful how you walk, not as unwise men but as wise, making the most of your time, because the days are evil. So then do not be foolish, but understand what the will of the Lord is" (Eph. 5:15-17).

We want to be wise, to lift our 24-hour days up to God with open hands in love. We don't want to be trying to see what pastimes or pleasures we'll be "allowed" to keep and "still follow God." We don't want to be like those who "walked after emptiness and became empty" (Jer. 2:5). We want to "walk as children of Light . . . in all goodness and righteousness and truth, trying to learn what is pleasing to the Lord" (Eph. 5:8-10). We want to be willing to turn aside from any delight the world has to offer if the Spirit is saying "not now" or perhaps "not ever."

Former missionary to India Amy Carmichael had some wise reflections on leisure time. "There is no harm in recreation—if you mean a pastime that will re-equip you for future work, and will not cause a leakage of spiritual power. We must have a fresh in-flooding of life for soul and body too, or we will dry up. The real question, however, is this: where are we to find our fresh springs of life? . . . Certain forms of 'recreation' [take] hold of us and hinder rather than help."[13]

My prayer: Lord, open my mind to your Spirit's direction on avenues of recreation that will truly re-create, renew, and refresh Your servant.

123

> Whom have I in heaven but You? And besides You, I desire nothing on earth. My flesh and my heart may fail, but God is the strength of my heart and my portion forever. (Ps. 73:25-26)

One evening I was making my way on foot to the corner of a very congested section of the city. ("Making my way" as there was no sidewalk, and the road was part of a busy night market, full of meandering pedestrians and motorcyclists.) As I reached the corner, two vehicles were blocking my passage, frozen as their drivers decided which could claim the right of way. Rather than wait, I decided to walk through a tiny parking lot on the corner; in the semi-darkness I could see that the one-lane entrance beside the guard's station was clear of traffic. No sooner did I start through than the heavy metal entrance bar swished past my body. I moved aside as I felt it, so I wasn't hurt. But I could have been, and I was both astonished and slightly angry with the guard. A passing pedestrian saw the incident and laughed. My bids for sympathy or an apology from the guard for not checking before lowering the mechanical arm got me nothing; the man was uninterested.

And by the grace of God, with the eyes of my spirit, I saw the "pit" open up before me. I could choose to embrace anger and blame these men for their cold hearts—and by doing so I would step away from the deep fellowship I had been enjoying with Christ. As I turned to walk home, I began pleading that God would keep me from the sin of unforgiveness, to please let me stay Jesus' friend. (He told His disciples, "You are my friends, if you do what I command you," and I had begun to taste something of that relationship.) God was faithful and cleansed me and revived me; I have never remembered the incident with anger or hurt—only with awe and gratitude.

Those who have gone before us testify that there is nothing which cannot be forgiven. Murderers have been forgiven by the victims' closest family members. Those who have suffered the horrors of concentration camps have forgiven their captors for the cruel treatment toward them personally, and even toward loved ones who died in the camps. The news is brought back to us again and again that yes, even in the midst of torture, it is possible to make one's way into the love of God and find safe refuge. Not safety from pain, but safety from evil, safety from sin.

Heart, Soul, Mind, and Strength

If I regard wickedness in my heart, the Lord will not hear; but certainly God has heard; He has given heed to the voice of my prayer. Blessed be God, who has not turned away my prayer nor His lovingkindness from me. (Ps. 66:18-20)

124

> Joseph was sold as a slave. They afflicted his feet with fetters, he himself was laid in irons; until the time that his word came to pass, the word of the Lord tested him. (Ps. 105: 17-19)

God has his own schools for perseverance. Paul described himself and his fellow workers as "servants of God, in much endurance, in afflictions, in hardships, in distresses, in beatings, in imprisonments, in tumults, in labors, in sleeplessness, in hunger . . ." (2 Cor. 6:4-5).

In many places in the world, men and women face torture, death, or long imprisonment for their faith. They suffer for refusing to worship the false gods of their societies, for daring to tell others about Jesus, for translating the Bible into a local language, for acting to save others' lives from the slaughter. By God's wonderful grace, many who survive these horrors have written accounts of His faithfulness in their prison years, and how they managed to persevere in love and obedience to Christ. Corrie ten Boom, imprisoned in a German concentration camp in World War II for hiding Jewish refugees, testified, "In the German camp, with all its horror, I found many prisoners who had never heard of Jesus Christ. If God had not used my sister Betsie and me to bring them to Him, they would never have heard of Him. Many died, or were killed, but many died with the name of Jesus on their lips. They were well worth all our suffering."[14]

Throughout history and still today, nations oppress and exterminate foreign nations or ethnic groups within their own boundaries, for reasons ranging from economic gain to madness. Individuals may for no just reason face cruel treatment and suffering that goes on and on. And one day it may be *us* suffering.

Job has been there before us, crying out to God at the injustice of it all. For a long time, he was unable to sense God's presence, but his faith remained strong:

> Behold, I go forward but He is not there, and backward, but I cannot perceive Him; when He acts on the left, I cannot behold Him; He turns on the right, I cannot see Him. But He knows the way I take; when He has tried me, I shall come forth as gold. My foot has held fast to His path; I have kept His way and not turned aside (Job 23:8-11).

125

> O Lord, my heart is not proud, nor my eyes haughty; nor do I involve myself in great matters, or in things too difficult for me. (Ps. 131:1-2)

It is a popularly accepted myth that the world has grown smaller. It hasn't grown smaller. What has happened is that the technology of mass communication has created a continual tsunami wave of information about a small portion of world events, which pours into our lives from newspapers, TV screens, and the Internet. The events we hear and read about range from local elections to celebrity scandals to mass suffering in places we're embarrassed to admit we couldn't locate on a map; and the breadth of coverage gives the illusion that we are getting all the really important knowledge about the nations of the world.

God calls us to love Him with all of our minds. To do that, we each need to ask His wisdom in dealing with the news flow. Some cultures accord high status to those who "keep up with" the news, and our pride may move us to devote hours each week to skimming news media, achieving nothing but a mind proud of its knowledge and the admiration of others.

The world is huge, complex, and full of suffering caused by powerful organizations and governments, by the sinful actions of individuals, and by natural disasters, disease, and death. We are called to stretch our perspective beyond ourselves, to love the "neighbors" that God sets before us as much as we love ourselves. But we are finite. Our minds cannot encompass the entire world. When they try, they are in danger of setting themselves up as little gods that we secretly worship and admire.

Love the Lord by humbly accepting exactly the roles He calls you to play with regard to the news coming in. Expect Him to limit your coverage, direct your focus, and involve you in action. Is He calling you to pray for the sufferers you're reading about? To become active in efforts to serve the orphans, the homeless, the oppressed? Step forward as He shows you to; and step backward when He shows you that this isn't a problem He has called you to solve, or even a situation He needs you to fully understand.

126

> Also the foreigners who join themselves to the Lord, to minister to Him, and to love the name of the Lord, to be His servants . . . even those I will bring to My holy mountain and make them joyful in My house of prayer. (Is. 56:6-7)

In the days when God instituted the Levitical priesthood, the men of the Jewish tribe of Levi were responsible for every detail of temple activities. Yet God did not leave the job of "ministering to Him" in the hands of the religious professionals. The prophet Isaiah made it clear that the most despised outsiders, even eunuchs, even foreigners, could join themselves to God and become full-fledged ministers in His house. (*His* house: not the Levites' house, and not even a house that was the exclusive property of God's chosen people.)

How was it that these ordinary people could minister? It was because the primary element of worship was never the rituals (circumcision, burnt offerings, special holy days) but the activities inside people's hearts. God repeatedly told His people that it was their hearts that needed circumcising, and that their offerings were an abomination to Him when they were a substitute for obedience.

Regardless of the way our particular churches are set up, with whatever hierarchy of leadership, all Christians are called "to minister to Him, to love the name of the Lord, to be His servants."

And so what might happen on a Sunday morning, or whenever it is that I join my Christian brothers and sisters in corporate worship? I love God by first giving myself entirely to Him that day as a servant to Him and His people. I look around and let God show me whom I can bless—assist, encourage, listen to, rejoice with, mourn with. As the church service begins, I pray for the speakers, song leaders, and others "in charge," pray for them to have hearts open to God's love and wisdom, hearts ready to reject pride and deception. During the singing, I minister to God with all my heart. As the service progresses, I listen as a servant for what the Holy Spirit is teaching me, while remaining alert for an emergency call to intercede.

I agree in my heart, and agree with joy, that I'm a servant of God in His house of prayer.

127

> By this we know that we love the children of God, when we love God and observe His commandments. For this is the love of God, that we keep His commandments; and His commandments are not burdensome. For whatever is born of God overcomes the world; and this is the victory that has overcome the world—our faith. (1 John 5:2-4)

Any body of Christians, whether a megachurch of thousands or "two or three gathered together in My name," is a mix of people who see things differently. Each individual has a unique personality, family background, past church experience (even within the same congregation), and preference for worship styles; each has weaknesses as well as strengths; all have blind spots, and some may harbor secret sins.

Under these circumstances, how awfully easy it is for annoyance and resentment to enter our hearts. How hard it is to obey God and love the children of God, we think, "if she's going to act like that," "if he refuses to see reason."

Yet on Jesus' last night with the disciples, He reiterated His command to "love one another, just as I have loved you" (John 15:12).

We honor the Lord by accepting that this commandment is possible, or Jesus wouldn't have commanded it. We confess our wrong attitudes, and we pray once again to set our eyes on things above, where Christ is. His ways and His plans far exceed our obsessions and resentments, and the Spirit moves our focus from irritating individuals to a larger view. Every directive from God's throne moves His people toward unity in love, love for God and each other. His commands take us out of ourselves, out of our own replays of past situations, away from our own ideas of how things "ought to be." They call us simultaneously to boldness and submission: submission to doing God's business instead of our own, as a bold warrior armed with the shield of faith.

> May the Lord direct your hearts into the love of God and into the steadfastness of Christ. (2 Thess. 3:5)

128

> Encourage one another day after day, as long as it is still called 'Today,' so that none of you will be hardened by the deceitfulness of sin. (Heb. 3:13)

> Let us consider how to stimulate one another to love and good deeds, not forsaking our own assembling together, as is the habit of some, but encouraging one another . . . . (Heb. 10:24-25)

Proverbs 13:20 teaches, "He who walks with wise men will be wise." This is an easy truth to understand. Wise friends give good counsel; as we meet difficult situations, the friends will point out aspects we hadn't noticed. Because they love us, they won't hesitate to challenge us if we seem to be heading towards error.

Years ago a young Christian decided that she would take on a weekend job in addition to her fulltime regular job, in order to meet a financial goal. As Nancy talked it over with me, she agreed that it was very unfortunate the job would mean she could no longer attend either Sunday church service or her Saturday fellowship group. We both saw that cutting out this precious time with fellow Christians would put Nancy in a vulnerable position. But we were also naïve: we thought that it was enough for her to understand that the position was a weak one, and that understanding the danger was enough to negate it.

Nancy took the job. Within six months, she became secretly engaged to a non-Christian man, married him quickly to avoid being talked out of it, and refused all contact with her former church friends. We were all heartsick.

The Holy Spirit is a marvelous Counselor. But we ourselves are not always listening very well in our prayer times, or perhaps we have let those good prayer habits ("temporarily," we tell ourselves) fall by the wayside. Thanks be to God that the Church, Christ's body, can be God's individual agents of righteousness and wisdom. Not too many years after Nancy's sad experience, I myself had taken to spending time with a fascinating new colleague. Since John wasn't a Christian, I never thought of our meals and strolls together as dating, because, I told myself, I would never date a non-Christian. One day I was chatting with a Christian pal on the phone about a rather special day I'd had with John, one ending in a friendly kiss. My friend's simple response came straight from the Lord: "You're playing with fire, you know. What if someone else were telling *you* this story?" I immediately recognized the truth and stepped away from the relationship.

Love God by honoring His commands about encouraging others and staying within earshot yourself.

129

> There is a time for every event under heaven—a time to give birth and a time to die . . . . A time to weep and a time to laugh; a time to mourn and a time to dance. (Eccl. 3: 1-2, 4)

> Rejoice with those who rejoice, and weep with those who weep. Be of the same mind toward one another; do not be haughty in mind, but associate with the lowly. Do not be wise in your own estimation. (Rom. 12:15-16)

Our church fellowship group included a lively young woman, a talented musician who loved serving on the worship team as singer and instrumentalist. Julie loved God, and it was clear that her prayer life included some exciting times in God's presence. It was clear because Julie would frequently show up with a glowing face, bursting to tell everyone how wonderful her experiences had been. It took me many years to figure out why Julie's bubbling often irritated rather than inspired me, or, if I was in a low mood, left me feeling even lower.

At that time, Julie had not yet learned the difference between the dynamics inside and outside the prayer closet. Like many of us, she assumed that speaking to others about the evidences of God's love toward her was not only appropriate but a way to give more glory to God. Yet not every event of our prayer times is meant to be shared. Paul had to admonish the Christians in the Corinthian church for making a similar error when it came to speaking in tongues. The ones with the gift enjoyed practicing it in the assembly, but with no one to interpret, the others were probably shrugging their shoulders and trying to be patient. Paul asked the speakers to control their outbursts, "For you are giving thanks well enough, but the other person is not edified" (1 Cor. 14:17).

As we grow in our love for God, He will give us exquisite experiences of His presence; and we must learn to hug them to ourselves, to save our ecstasy for the prayer closet. If and when we ever speak of those experiences, it needs to be out of love for others, and not from a desire to show off. And we won't often be speaking of such things, because as God leads us to love others, we'll be striving to "be of the same mind" towards them—to feel their sorrows and celebrate their happiness. As we give up our desire to chat about our own doings, and listen to others speak of theirs, God can pour His love through us, and do more wonderful works.

130

> "This is My commandment, that you love one another, just as I have loved you." (John 15:12)

> "And the glory which You have given Me I have given to them, that they may be one, just as We are one; I in them, and Thou in Me, that they may be perfected in unity, that the world may know that You sent Me, and loved them, even as You loved Me." (John 17:22-23)

If we've ever paid attention to the final words of a person facing death, let's listen to our Lord Jesus. One of His last commands to His disciples, and His last prayer before His arrest, were both about Christians loving other Christians.

All heaven must weep over the deep divisions among us over the role of women in the church; over our understanding of the celebration of "the Lord's Supper," and how we practice it; over how we understand baptism, and how we practice it; over how we understand spiritual gifts and how we practice them. The tragedy is not that we have different opinions on these things and act accordingly. The tragedy is that we mock other Christians, despise other Christians, refuse the hand of fellowship because they disagree with us over these issues. Yet these issues are matters of scriptural interpretation unrelated either to sin or to the deity of Christ.

So why are we up in arms? It's not love motivating us when we laugh among church friends at the practices of other believers, or smugly shake our heads at their ways. It is pride in our presumed knowledge: we're right, and they are wrong, wrong, wrong. Our certainty becomes a god to us, and we neglect the foremost command of the true God. Yet scripture teaches, "If I have the gift of prophecy, and know all mysteries and all knowledge; if I have all faith, so as to remove mountains, but do not have love, I am nothing" (1 Cor. 13:2).

To strive with everything in us to love the family of God, it may help to understand some of the far-reaching tentacles of our lack of unity. Liu Zenying has written of the tremendous blessing it was when foreign Christians began to smuggle Bibles into China during the 1980s. "However," he wrote, "after a few years these same mission organizations started putting other books at the top of the bags of Bibles. These were books about one particular denomination's theology, or teaching that focused on certain aspects of God's Word. This, I believe, was the start of disunity among China's house churches . . . . The churches started to split into groups that believed one thing against groups that believed another."[15]

Let the Holy Spirit speak to your heart about loving God by loving His family.

131

> Be gracious to us, O Lord, be gracious to us, for we are greatly filled with contempt. Our soul is greatly filled with the scoffing of these who are at ease, with the contempt of the proud." (Ps. 123:3-4)

A children's chant says, "Sticks and stones may break my bones, but words will never hurt me," but adults learn that the second statement is wishful thinking. If only our gossip, fault-finding, boasting, and other words that denigrate others, which we later repent of, could have dissipated, simply polluting the air a bit. But they didn't. Adults know that words can be poison arrows: they not only wound, but inflict the hearer with the venomous feelings of the one who spoke them. The wounded one may shoot right back with his own evil arrow; or he may slowly be infected with hatred, resentment, and a desire for revenge.

How seriously can such feelings poison the soul? Proverbs 8:19 says, "A brother offended is harder to be won than a strong city, and contentions are like the bars of a citadel." This carries a strong warning about taking care not to offend our brother, but there's a second lesson here. When we ourselves accept the sinful words or action of others into our souls, we can end up in a spiritual prison. The cell will be dark, filled with the echoes of the words that have hurt us; before we realize it, we'll be avoiding any contact with those who caused us pain, or we'll be planning subtle ways to punish them for not valuing us.

When we are walking close to the Lord, we can avoid being decimated by poison arrows. We can pull them right out, take our pain and sorrow to the Lord, and receive His comfort. We can forgive and bless those who chose to act like enemies, whether it was done with deliberation or in a moment's foolish decision.

When we don't act quickly and only later realize that we're choking to death in a cell filled with contempt for others, we must cry out to God, like the writer of the psalm above. Only God can rescue us, and restore our souls. Then we can obey the command of love once again.

132

Henry the Fifth of England was a just and godly king. History records that when he and his soldiers won the decisive Battle of Agincourt against France outnumbered by 6:1 odds, Henry refused to lead a victory parade; he wanted all glory to go to God.

In Shakespeare's play *Henry V*, three of the kings' associates, one a close friend, conspire to betray him. The plot is discovered, but the conspirators aren't yet aware of it. Though the men deserve death, the king is determined to give them a chance to receive mercy instead. He engages the three in a casual conversation. He tells them of a drunken fellow in the town who was shouting insults about the king; Henry laughs and suggests that the man's foolish raving would best be overlooked. The three men react with protests in defense of Henry's honor—surely, they say, the man should be whipped. "Yet let there be mercy!" Henry pleads. The men reiterate their judgment—the fellow should receive the punishment he deserves.

In sorrow and anger, King Henry tells the conspirators that they have sealed their own fate. Their treachery is known, and the guards in the room are there to escort them to a place of punishment.

This scene is a perfect metaphor of the choice offered to Christians throughout their lives on earth. We know the words of the Lord's Prayer. Will we betray our Master again and again through withholding mercy to others? If so, then we must expect no mercy ourselves.

Let's always remember Jesus' teaching about the law of love.

> For if you forgive others for their transgressions, your heavenly Father will also forgive you. But if you do not forgive others, then your Father will not forgive your transgressions. (Matt. 6:14-15)

133

> The seventy returned with joy, saying, "Lord, even the demons are subject to us in Your name." And He said to them, "... I have given you authority to tread on serpents and scorpions, and over all the power of the enemy, and nothing will injure you. Nevertheless, do not rejoice in this, that the spirits are subject to you, but rejoice that your names are recorded in heaven." (Luke 10:17-20)

The seventy disciples that Jesus had sent out to cities and towns in advance of His own visits had just had the most electrifying weeks of their lives. Yet Jesus was telling them they were not to rejoice in the fact that God's power in them recently had (and would continue to have) demons on the run.

I wonder if the men were puzzled. They were exhilarated, undoubtedly lifting up lots of praise to God for the amazing acts of power they had seen. Why would Jesus be calming them down? Of course, the truth that their names were recorded in heaven might have been amazing news to them. Before Jesus spoke, they may not have known this fact. But today we Christians do know it, and it's hard not to notice a discrepancy in the levels of excitement we feel about the two things. Compared with confronting demons and winning, having an eternal standing in Christ seems very bland and tame—though discovering that attitude in our minds may embarrass us.

Many of us have had the heady experience of being a part of exciting works that God was doing, followed by weeks that ranged from dull to extremely discouraging. Surely one reason is because we've kept recalling and rejoicing again and again in the wonderful things that occurred; and imperceptibly we've moved *away* from looking to King Jesus. We're no longer looking to Him to receive today's words for today's works. We're reluctant to let the past pass, because it was indeed sweet and thrilling. Yet when we cling to the past, we are no longer clinging to Jesus.

In the above scripture, the Lord teaches clearly that we must disengage. After we have praised God from the depths of our souls, and testified to others (in ways He directs us), we should deliberately calm down. We may require a good rest! And then we must direct our hearts and minds to what is needful: God's manna for the new day.

God wants so much to give His children all they need to walk in His ways of love and service. "Open your mouth wide and I will fill it.... I would feed you with the finest of the wheat, and with honey from the rock I would satisfy you" (Ps. 81:10, 16).

134

> Only give heed to yourself and keep your soul diligently, so that you do not forget the things which your eyes have seen and they do not depart from your heart all the days of your life; but make them known to your sons and your grandsons. (Deut. 4:9)

Earlier I referred to a period of my life where I faced the loss of a job I had held for eighteen years. During that time of uncertainty about the future, God showed me how much I'd come to depend on this particular organization and our reciprocal relationship—they valued my skills and paid me for them, and I enjoyed the work I did. In my view, it was a perfect set-up. Now, for complicated official reasons, it was going to end.

Around this time, I attended an art exhibition at which I bought a small oil painting entitled "Broken Boat Blues." It depicted a small sailboat broken in two in a swirling sea, its owner floundering in the waves. I was reminded of Jonah; God arranged to get him thrown off a ship going in the wrong direction, after which Jonah got whale transport back to where he could journey on foot in the direction God had commanded. In short, God had plans for Jonah that involved first getting him off the ship. The broken boat in the painting also reminded me that nothing on earth can be our rock, the thing we ultimately depend on. Jobs disappear; friends and loved ones move away, die; war devastates nations.

I purchased "Broken Boat Blues" and hung it in my house. Seeing it reminds me that boats break, and that every circumstance that gets me floundering in the waves can drive me closer to the God I'm meant to cling to.

This painting also becomes a topic of conversation with those who visit my home. I tell them of how God worked in my heart during that period of my life, and of the truths that the picture brings to my mind. I want to live in the present, not the past. But I don't want the things which my eyes have seen to "slip from my heart" as the NIV Bible expresses it.

Journals, photos, souvenirs, scrapbooks, songs, poems, memorials, celebrations, anniversaries (like the Passover was)—all are ways we might respond to the scripture above. Let the Holy Spirit show you how to love God by remembering the mighty works He has done.

135

> "I am eighty-five years old today. I am still as strong today as I was in the day Moses sent me; as my strength was then, so my strength is now, for war and for going out and for coming in. Now then, give me this hill country about which the Lord spoke on that day, for you heard on that day that the Anakim were there, with great fortified cities; perhaps the Lord will be with me, and I will drive them out as the Lord has spoken." (Josh. 14:10-12)

Caleb, who spoke the words above, was one of twelve leaders who was sent to spy out the land of Canaan forty-five years earlier; only he and Joshua had brought back courageous and encouraging reports, and the rebellious congregation of Israelites had threatened to stone the two of them. Looking back, Caleb could recall, "I followed the Lord my God fully," and rather than retire, Caleb was standing in readiness, as perhaps the Lord would use him in His plans once more.

The Bible has lots of examples of men and women who served God with courage, faithfulness, and perseverance. But scripture only gives us the highlights. When it comes to their daily lives, much is left to our imaginations.

As one who has had little practice in either courage or perseverance, and yearns for models, I'll recommend something that has been very helpful for me: reading biographies and autobiographies of individuals whose lives have demonstrated these qualities. As I read, dividing the admirable from the less worthy in the lives of imperfect people, I find myself studying their lifestyles, their habits, their ways of thinking. I notice their personal mottos, their response to setbacks, their ways of keeping themselves on track.

In the autobiography referred to earlier in this book, Pete Goss wrote that after reaching the decision to eventually compete in a single-handed round-the-world race, he deliberately let his goal determine his subsequent choices. "From now on," he wrote, "every decision I took outside my private life would be based on that ambition. Whenever I was faced with a choice, I would only have to ask myself what was in the best interests of my goal and a clear answer would usually present itself."[16]

The sailor's words have given me a practical application for the scripture below, which of course includes my private life as well:

Let us also lay aside every encumbrance and the sin which so easily entangles us, and let us run with endurance the race that is set before us, fixing our eyes on Jesus, the author and perfecter of faith . . . . (Heb. 12:1-2)

136

> The Lord also spoke to Moses, saying, "Speak to the sons of Israel, and tell them that they shall make for themselves tassels on the corners of their garments throughout their generations.... And it shall be a tassel for you to look at and remember all the commandments of the Lord, so as to do them and not follow after your own heart and your own eyes, after which you played the harlot, in order that you may remember to do all My commandments, and be holy to your God." (Num. 15:37-40)

When God spoke these words for the people He had rescued from cruel slavery in Egypt, they had already lived in the wilderness for about two years. Moses repeated God's promises to faithfully support them, and explained the honor and obedience God required of them, and the laws and procedures He wanted them to follow. Meanwhile, God provided. Abundant manna appeared six days a week, and the people knew to gather it in advance for the Sabbath, the day of rest. Their clothes were holding up—they would not deteriorate for forty years. God's presence among the people was constantly tangible; for those who wanted to go and take a look and reassure themselves, the miraculous cloud always hovered over the tent of meeting.

During those two years, the Israelites "played the harlot" several times, God's metaphor for idolatry. The creation of the golden calf was an obvious instance, but after that time the disloyalty to God had taken the form of rebellion. ("For rebellion is as the sin of divination, and insubordination is as iniquity and idolatry" [1 Sam. 15:23].) The people had begun to complain bitterly about the monotony of the manna, actually weeping with frustration. Scripture records that "the rabble who were among them had greedy desires," or literally "desired a desire." Their determination to get what they wanted, a tasty hunk of meat, overcame their reverence for their Provider. This was just the beginning of further breakouts of rebellion among God's chosen people. Moses' siblings complained about God's distribution of authority; the entire congregation, when it was time to enter the promised land of Canaan and fight for it, let their fear of the tall Canaanites overwhelm them, and some counseled mutiny.

God punished them. And later, the Lord was so sure the Israelites had not learned their painful lesson that he had them sew tassels on their clothes to remind them: Don't make gods of the desires you find in your heart; don't covet power, or things I haven't chosen to give you. Remember My commands and do them.

The rallying cry of the world is "Self-realization, self-empowerment, self-fulfillment!" We must reject these cries and listen only to our Lord.

> "I am the Lord your God who brought you out from the land of Egypt to be your God; I am the Lord your God" (Num. 15:41).

137

> O God, You are my God; I shall seek You earnestly; my soul thirsts for You, my flesh yearns for You, in a dry and weary land where there is no water. Thus I have seen You in the sanctuary, to see Your power and Your glory.... My soul is satisfied as with marrow and fatness, and my mouth offers praises with joyful lips. (Ps. 63: 1-2, 5)

In 1983, Air Canada Flight 143 took off from Montreal bound for Edmonton without enough fuel to get there. The ground crew had become confused in measuring the amounts of fuel for the new twin-engine 767, and the plane's computer was out of order. When the pumps delivering fuel to the engines began failing, the pilots diagnosed the problem and by God's grace managed to reach an unused airfield in time to avert a tragedy. Long before the aircraft reached the runway, its two engines had stopped and the plane had become a glider. In the movie made of the incident, the captain commented that it was as if the plane were "running on fumes."

In our eagerness to serve God with all our strength, we are often in the position of those pilots. We have places to go, schedules to keep, and we make do with a glance at surface appearances. Are our clothes appropriate? Is the room tidy? Is the food ready? Are the handouts prepared? Are people where they're supposed to be? Are the sound system and computers working?

Yet unless we have spent time drinking from the Source of all our strength, until our thirsty souls are filled to the brim, we are courting disaster. We'll be running on fumes. We're unlikely to reach our real destination at all. And no matter how satisfactory things appear to others, we will know that we haven't delighted the One Person who matters the most.

To borrow the metaphor of the plane once more, let's not offer service to God that is accomplished by choking engines, engines that have no business being off the ground in that condition. Let's do whatever it takes to set our lives aright, so that we are offering God vessels well-filled with His strength to do His tasks.

> Ascribe strength to God; His majesty is over Israel and His strength is in the skies. O God, You are awesome from Your sanctuary. The God of Israel Himself gives strength and power to the people. Blessed be God! (Ps. 68: 34-35)

138

> Jesus answered and said to her, "Everyone who drinks of this water will thirst again; but whoever drinks of the water that I will give him shall never thirst; but the water that I will give him will become in him a well of water springing up to eternal life." (John 4:13-14)

Jesus lived in an era without plumbing. People who wanted water had to haul it from wells. When the above conversation takes place, Jesus has been sitting at a well alone; He doesn't have the necessary equipment for drawing water, so He asks a local woman to give Him a drink when she herself comes to the well to draw some.

As He often does, Jesus turns the conversation to spiritual things, from a physical liquid to a spiritual substance. This physical liquid will satisfy people only briefly; then they will become thirsty again and have to travel a distance to the well to haul up more. But Jesus speaks of giving people spiritual "water" which itself becomes a well inside them; the water is there, always there, ready to be drunk.

Restless, bored, lonely, troubled souls turn everywhere for rest, delight, companionship, and peace. Some things never satisfy at all, and nothing ever satisfies for long. But Jesus' words tell Christians that for a drink of living water they needn't go anywhere at all. Even imprisoned in a prison cell the size of a closet, the well of life is there within them. Jesus is there, within them. They only need to turn to Him and drink.

When the disciples return to the well where they left their master, they urge Him to eat the food they've brought back. And scripture records another precious comparison between physical and spiritual sustenance. "I have food to eat that you do not know about," Jesus tells the men. "My food is to do the will of Him who sent Me and to accomplish His work" (John 4: 32, 34).

Jesus' words offer us two permanent signposts along the path to a deeper love for the Father, a love like His own. When we are in need of the slightest mental or emotional refreshment, we are to turn inside and drink from the well of Christ. And instead of making it life's first priority to please our stomachs and taste buds, we're to be like Jesus. We're to listen for God's instructions for the day, the hour, the moment, with the intention of obeying them.

139

One day, after a productive morning of working at home on lesson plans for my evening classes, I was walking briskly to the subway station. As I rounded a corner, I came across a well-dressed old woman with two bulging shopping bags. In her heavy coat, she was over-dressed for a day which had turned quite warm, and she had paused on the sidewalk, almost motionless, her face unnaturally red. She seemed to look beseechingly, in pain, right at me. In retrospect, I think she was heading home from her shopping when she suddenly experienced exhaustion, possibly even heart or other trouble. And I might have offered to scoop up her burdens and get her home.

What I did instead was look at her from the mental fog of my pressing future plans for the day. I figured I would get to the office and complete the workbook corrections and other tasks I'd calculated could be finished in the time before my classes began. Sad to remember, I walked on.

Once again, my heavenly Father reminded me of the old lesson: to love Him in the present, the now, and be ready to "listen as a disciple." Had I been in an attitude of prayer-without-ceasing as I walked my route, I might have heard a word telling me to help the woman. Or I might have *asked* God's will for me in this situation as I recognized her need.

The experience illuminated another view of the parable of the good Samaritan. Those who passed by the injured man may have been good-hearted, well-intentioned people, but God and they were not *currently* abiding in a close love relationship. Perhaps, as with me, their good intentions were all about their preset agendas. They had temporarily become the little gods of their day, of their journey from Point X to Point Y. So they missed hearing God's wisdom, and they missed an opportunity to pour out their love to God in obedience.

> Blessed is the man who listens to me, watching daily at my gates, waiting at my doorposts. For he who finds me finds life and obtains favor from the Lord. (Prov. 8:34-35)

140

When I have been living far from God (if it can be called living), separated by sins and my own reluctance to deal with them in His presence, one of Jesus' parables is a great comfort.

> A man had two sons, and he came to the first and said, "Son, go to work today in the vineyard." And he answered, "I will not"; but afterward he regretted it and went. The man came to the second and said the same thing; and he answered, "I will, sir"; but he did not go. Which of the two did the will of his father? (Matt. 21: 28-31)

Jesus' listeners give the right answer: the former.

If we were perfect children and servants, faithful friends of our dear Lord, we would always get it just right. We would daily, and throughout the day, say "I will, Lord," and proceed to do what He told us to. We would reject all temptations to entertain those sins of the mind and heart that would stop love's flow to others and cause us to hide from God. If we fell, we would repent quickly, pick ourselves up, and get back on the path.

We aren't perfect children. But according to the scriptures, God cares more about endings than beginnings. Righteous people who stop honoring God and turn to lives of sin are held accountable for Act Two of their lives. Likewise, "if a wicked man turns from all his sins which he has committed and observes all My statutes and practices justice and righteousness, he shall live; he shall not die" (Ezek. 18:21).

Most Christians are flabbergasted to read of how God forgave King Ahab when he repented. This was the king whom scripture records did more evil than all the previous kings of Israel.

God's love and forgiveness are awesome. From a human viewpoint, His justice seems incredibly unfair—in our favor! When we have wandered off the path for any period of time, let's not lose our desire to be back in the Shepherd's arms.

141

> For from the days of old they have not heard or perceived by ear, nor has the eye seen a God besides You, who acts in behalf of the one who waits for Him. You meet him who rejoices in doing righteousness, who remembers You in Your ways. (Is. 64:4-5)

Isaiah's long prophetic message is addressed to a rebellious nation which has fallen away from faithfulness to a faithful God. God alternately admonishes, warns, and pleads with His people, "a rebellious people, who walk in the way which is not good, following their own thoughts, a people who continually provoke Me to My face" (Is. 65:2-3). Isaiah says of them, "And there is no one who calls on Your name, who arouses himself to take hold of You" (64:7).

But thanks be to God, those words don't describe *us*. If they did once, they don't anymore. We *have* aroused ourselves to take hold of God. We're seeking to love Him with all that is in us, seeking to walk in *His* ways instead of our own.

So the promise in Isaiah 64:4-5 is for us. As we wait on God, as we rejoice in doing the righteous things He shows us to do, as we deliberately look to Him for guidance—He meets us, and He acts for us and in us.

These truths are so amazing that we can only shake our heads in wonder and rejoice daily with our hearts, our voices, and our lives.

> How blessed are the people who know the joyful sound! O Lord, they walk in the light of Your countenance. In Your name they rejoice all the day and by Your righteousness they are exalted. (Ps. 89:15-16)

142

> How blessed is the man whose strength is in You, in whose heart are the highways to Zion! Passing through the valley of Baca they make it a spring; the early rain also covers it with blessings. They go from strength to strength, every one of them appears before God in Zion. (Ps. 84:5-7)

And now for a personal testimony, the story behind this book. I grew up in a Christian culture and came to faith in Christ as a teenager. That faith didn't stand the strain of the intellectual and emotional struggles of young adulthood, but the Lord led me back to Himself when I was in my twenties.

My life after that was no great Christian success story. In fact, it was filled with the ups and downs of struggling with my pet sins, namely those associated with chronic perfectionism: criticism and judgment. (I hadn't yet learned the lessons in this book of keeping my mind clear so that the Spirit of God could operate there.) Meanwhile I was involved in church activities, reading the Bible, trying to learn how to walk in God's ways.

Then, when I was in my forties, my father died of cancer. I was hit by a deep sadness and loss of energy that went on and on. My life as a teacher and editor continued as usual, my apartment remained clean and tidy, my aerobic exercise schedule was unchanged. But I began to believe a lie.

The lie was this: "I have no more energy left for dealing with the struggles of living the Christian life. No matter how hard I've tried, I haven't gotten past the critical attitudes that destroy relationships and ministries. God will just have to change me one day." In short, I believed I had no strength.

Nearly seven dry, barren years went by. Proverbs 14:14 says it all: "The backslider in heart will have his fill of his own ways." One day I picked up a copy of the Inter-Varsity Press classic *This Morning with God: A Daily Study Guide to the Entire Bible* and began getting into the scriptures once again. Within days I was reading the words, "You shall love the Lord your God with all your heart, and with all your soul, and with all your strength, and with all your mind; and your neighbor as yourself" (Luke 10:27).

And the Holy Spirit began speaking truth to my heart. I realized that God would not command His people to do something they could not do. This commandment presupposed that I had a heart, a soul, a mind ... and strength! Yes, I had *always* had strength. The job I performed, the home I kept up, and the physical health I maintained all testified to my having had much more strength than I knew. I simply hadn't offered up that strength to my God—not all of it, not *any* of it.

"I never knew, I never knew!" cried my soul, and I began chasing the words "strength" and "heart" and "soul" and "mind" all through the Bible, especially in the scriptures already around in Jesus' day, to see if they could tell me what it might mean to love God with all I had in me. This began my quest, and eventually God opened up other scriptures related to loving and obeying Him. And at a certain point it became clear that these lessons needed to be shared with the family of God.

I sincerely hope the reflections in this devotional have been used by our Father to help you love Him more. My final offering to the family is an alternate version of our classic children's hymn.

> **Jesus loves me, this I know**
> **For the Bible tells me so**
> **Little ones to Him belong**
> **And in Jesus they are strong!**

May you go on from strength to strength.

Notes

[1] Rebecca Manley Pippert, *Hope Has Its Reasons* (HarperCollins Publishers, New York, 1989), p. 183.

[2] *Crudens Complete Concordance* (Zondervan Publishing House, 1968), p. 505.

[3] Stephen R. Covey, *The 7 Habits of Highly Effective People* (Free Press, A Division of Simon & Shuster, Inc., New York, 1989).

[4] Joni Eareckson Tada, *A Quiet Place in a Crazy World* (Multnomah Books, Oregon, 1993), p. 68.

[5] Elizabeth Alves, *Becoming a Prayer Warrior* (Gospel Light/Regal Books, Ventura, CA, 1998), p. 16.

[6] Ibid., pp. 75-76.

[7] "I nod on to a million visions," *The Observer*, November 8, 1987.

[8] Christopher Nolan, *Under the Eye of the Clock* (Orion Books Ltd, London, 1999), p. 148.

[9] *Have You Heard of the Four Spiritual Laws?* (Campus Crusade for Christ, Inc., Orlando, Florida, 1965, 1994), p. 1.

[10] Used by permission of *Discipleship Journal,* Copyright © July/August 2006, The Navigators. Used by permission of NavPress. All rights reserved.

[11] Brother Yun and Paul Hattaway, *The Heavenly Man* (Monarch Books, London, 2002), p. 267.

[12] Paul R. McReynolds, *Word Study Greek English New Testament* (Tyndale House Publishers, Inc. 1999), p. 704.

[13] Amy Carmichael, *God's Missionary* (Christian Literature Crusade, Pennsylvania, 1997), pp. 3-4.

[14] Corrie ten Boom, *Tramp for the Lord* (Fleming H. Revell Company, New Jersey, 1976), p. 12.

[15] Yun and Hattaway, p. 233.

[16] Pete Goss, *Close to the Wind* (Headline Book Publishing, London, 1998), p. 22.

FOR GROUP DISCUSSION AND PRAYER

(Questions correspond with the numbers of the devotional readings.)

1. What amazes you about the phenomenal body God has given you?
2. What do you and a potted plant have in common? What are some big differences?
3. What is your past experience of reading the Bible?
4. What are your earliest memories of praying? How have your prayers changed over the years?
5. "Jesus is the host with infinitely more to offer." What has Jesus sometimes offered you?
6. Have you ever asked God to help you understand a particular section of scripture?
7. Share another example from the natural world which has made you marvel.
8. Why is human loyalty sometimes "like the dew which goes away early"?
9. Share a song or psalm which speaks praise to God.
10. Choose a section of Psalm 119 to use as a prayer.
11. Rev. 5:12 says that Jesus is worthy to receive power, riches, wisdom, might, honor, glory, and blessing. Is there anything you are withholding?
12. Whom have you withheld forgiveness from, and what will you do about it?
13. Confess your bitterness toward particular individuals and accept prayer for God's healing of your heart.
14. Is there something you have said "Yes, Lord" about but failed to follow through on?
15. Share strategies for keeping pure.
16. What are some habits that keep your body strong? How about your mind? And your spirit?
17. Which commands in the Bible have you found difficult, even impossible, but now accept as possible to obey?
18. What particular "good works" is God asking you to walk in, with the strength you are being given?
19. Praise God aloud as you recall mountain or sea experiences, or as you look at photos or videos of these scenes.

20. Is there a situation that you might be struggling with because of your limited angle of vision?
21. What situation will develop if we don't let Jesus wash our dirty feet?
22. Have you been remembering to keep the main thing the main thing? What have been some results?
23. Is there a sin God wants confessed and cut out of your life?
24. In what ways might our pursuit of a deeper love for God be as demanding as our jobs?
25. On a scale of one to ten, how much do you enjoy reading the Bible?
26. Pray for a softer heart toward some hard-to-love people in your life.
27. How does church music affect you?
28. Memorize Psalm 94:18-19 together.
29. "Speak of all His wonders." Share a recent "wonder" that God has performed in your life or another's.
30. As a group, try short prayers together on a single subject. One person introduces the subject by a single-sentence prayer. (For example, "Lord, we lift up Mark, as he awaits surgery on his heart.") One by one, others add details to that prayer, no more than one or two sentences per person. (One person might pray for the doctor's skill and wisdom, another for Mark's anxious family members, another for Mark's swift recovery.) When no one else has a bit to add, the subject is considered "covered" and a new topic is introduced.
31. What have you done this past week to renew your spirit's strength?
32. Did you try using the prayer idea from Joni? How did it go?
33. Share your success with swatting ugly thoughts away this past week.
34. Like the author, have you had the experience of seeing yourself grow physically stronger? Did this make the "tedious" routines worth the effort?
35. What rich and nutritious wisdom has the Lord fed you with most recently?
36. Are your Sundays restful?
37. How much practice have you had in walking in yoke with Jesus?
38. What has the Holy Spirit been showing you about God's commands to rest?
39. Have you started recording what God has been teaching you, or what He's been doing in your life?
40. Do you have the habit of chatting with God? Have you "caught" some of His thoughts to you?

Affirmations

Affirmations are positive statements of Truth. Each time we pray affirmatively, we are lifted into a consciousness of Oneness, calling forth the divine activity within us.

May

Inner Peace	I am at peace.
Guidance	I open my heart to infinite wisdom.
Healing	I am healthy in mind, body, and spirit.
Prosperity	I affirm my divine inheritance and claim my good.
World Peace	I envision peace, harmony, and love for all people.

June

Inner Peace	The peace of God permeates my being.
Guidance	Answers come to me in the Silence.
Healing	I radiate health, harmony, and wholeness.
Prosperity	The blessings of God fill my life, and I am prosperous.
World Peace	Peace on earth begins with me.

DAILY WORD®

A Unity Publication

Laura Harvey, Editor | Vol. 151 | No. 5 | May/June 2013

Annual cover price: $35.70 a year (U.S.A.) Single copy: $5.95

1 Affirmations

4 A Breath of Joy—
Elliott Robertson

6 Transcendent Love—
Bertha Sánchez, LUT

10 Your Letters

11 Daily Messages for May

43 Daily Messages for June

44 The Faith of a Child—
Roxanne Daleo, Ph.D.

Cover © Thinkstock

Reader Alert

Unauthorized parties may attempt to solicit your new or renewal subscription to *Daily Word*. Be sure to start or renew your order through:

- Our websites: *www.dailyword.com* or *www.shopunity.org*.
- Renewal notices with the *Daily Word* logo and Lee's Summit, MO address.

Have questions or need help with your subscription?

Please call Customer Care at
1-800-669-0282
(International: 01-816-969-2069)
Monday-Friday
7:30 a.m.-4:30 p.m. (CT)

Daily Word is published bimonthly by Unity, 1901 NW Blue Parkway, Unity Village, MO 64065-0001. Circulation Management - Circulation Specialists, Inc. Annual cover price is $35.70 a year in the U.S.A. and possessions.

Unity cannot be held responsible for loss or damage to unsolicited materials.

From time to time we make our mailing lists available to selected, reputable organizations that may be of interest to our readers. If you do not want to receive these mailings, please contact our Customer Care department.

Canada BN 13252 9033 RT   © 2013 by Unity. All rights reserved.

unity®
A positive path
for spiritual living

41. Have you been changing some of the ways you use "down time" since you started pursuing obedience to the two great commandments?
42. Read Psalm 145 aloud as a prayer.
43. Share your thoughts on the dialog between Jesus and Peter in John 21.
44. Do you know Christians whose Christlike qualities point you to Jesus, not themselves?
45. How can you help Christian friends who regularly indulge in fault-finding or judgment?
46. What does it mean to "listen as a disciple"?
47. Have you ever had a long, lazy period of hanging out with Jesus? Could you have these times more often?
48. Why do you think that God values humility so highly in His servants?
49. Share a time when God used your "answer of the tongue" to unexpectedly bless others.
50. When you read the parable of the Prodigal Son, do you identify yourself more with the elder brother or the younger one?
51. When did you become a Christian?
52. Share a song that speaks wonderful truths about God and His promises.
53. What happens when we forget that our hearts can't be set on cruise control?
54. Plan a thanksgiving party. While enjoying refreshments, you might circle the group three times, having people share in turn about how God has blessed them: first, through their family; next, in their job or school situation; finally, in their church setting. (Or choose three other ways to keep the thanks specific. For instance, thanks for a particular challenge of the past year; thanks for a person God has used in your life; thanks for a lesson God has taught you.)
55. Is there a "natural tendency" which you have used as an excuse for sin?
56. What is your experience, if any, of hearing God's voice and knowing it?
57. What kinds of songs usually come into your mind? Do you sing them out?
58. Does "love boomerang" express your experience of the past weeks? Do you want to keep playing? How much do you want it?
59. Is God calling you to make specific changes in your life in order to devote more hours and energy to His concerns?
60. What has God shown you this week about Himself and His ways through a section of scripture you read?

61. Is Jesus the head of your house?
62. Pray that you will treasure conversations with your dear Lord more than your food.
63. Has God shown you that you've withheld forgiveness from someone recently? Have you obeyed Him yet?
64. Has God ever explicated a verse of scripture for you?
65. How does it feel to know that you wear the crown of lovingkindness and compassion?
66. Are you used to referring to commentaries and "study Bibles" when you read the scriptures?
67. Read Judges, chapters six through eight. What stands out for you in this account?
68. Have you ever asked God for confirmation when you weren't sure where an idea or voice came from?
69. Has the Lord shown you a formidable task He wants you to do?
70. Do you know of other "functionally weak" children of God through whom God has brought glory to Himself?
71. Does anyone in the group need encouragement to do the good works that God might be calling them to walk in?
72. Have you sensed that you're a part of one, or several, of God's plans? Is this something God wants you to share or to keep to yourself?
73. Share a time you were encouraged unexpectedly by someone you only met once in your life.
74. Has poverty seemed frightening to you? Humiliating? Ugly?
75. Pray for willingness to give God complete charge of your time, talents, and wealth.
76. Share examples of how "seed" you were given was both "bread" to eat and "seed" to plant.
77. Nebuchadnezzar fell into the sin of pride by reflecting on the greatness of the city he had built. What tempts you to self-worship? (Be careful how you share, that it doesn't become boasting.) Pray for each other about not falling into pride.
78. Have you ever received God's comfort through another person?
79. Share your experience with inviting friends to Christian meetings.
80. Have you become bolder in recent weeks? Share examples.
81. What are some of "the world's paths" that God has shown you to avoid?
82. Has a long experience of waiting for God to change circumstances taught you humility?
83. Has God ever woken you up at night?

84. Is there any "furniture" God has asked you to get rid of?
85. Have you ever turned your mind from terror and looked on God? What was the result?
86. As God's priests, pray for the family members of those in your group.
87. Why does an hour or two of reading a Christian book or seeing a Christian movie sometimes attract us more than an hour or two of private time with God?
88. Share books that have helped you to grasp the essence of perseverance.
89. Read the first eight chapters of Nehemiah. Share what God teaches you.
90. Use each scripture in this devotional reading as a starting point in group prayer.
91. What is the balance between "I can do all things through Christ who strengthens me" and "He gives His beloved sleep"?
92. Use your imagination. What might Peterson have meant when he said that keeping a weekly Sabbath impacted his marriage, children, church life, friendships, and writing?
93. Pray for anyone in the group who gets trapped by wanting things to be perfect.
94. Have you ever been grateful for God's correction?
95. Whom will you intercede for as a group this week?
96. Did anyone consciously put on God's armor this week?
97. Read 1 Corinthians 10:13. Share an experience when God showed you a way of escape from sexual temptation.
98. What compromises does the Evil One tempt Christians to make today in order to stay "current"?
99. What has been your usual response to pain? Do you bury it by excessive behavior? Flee from situations? Roll up your soul like an armadillo to avoid being hurt again?
100. Pray for willingness to obey God's directives—both general scriptural ones and personal ones—about the worthless things in your life.
101. Share a particular disappointment which God taught you to be grateful about.
102. Should Christians try to seem more joyful than they feel?
103. Do you know a person who is a great example of a reconciler?
104. Pray for people you know who are fighting difficult battles.
105. Put yourself in David's shoes. How do you think David was able to avoid choosing bitterness?

106. On a scale of one to ten, how well are you doing in obeying God's command to rest? Did God use anything in this reading to speak to you personally?
107. Pray for Christians experiencing persecution.
108. Has God revealed cowardice in any areas of your life? Pray for each other.
109. Did God use this reading as reminder this week, so that "idly thinking" about someone turned into praying for them?
110. Do any attributes of Peter remind you of yourself?
111. Have you ever found "wealth" (of any amount) to be a trap?
112. Does the "Me" diagram illustrate your own worldview? Is that worldview changing?
113. Has God ever gotten your attention in a surprising way?
114. Pray for the leaders of the church(es) represented in your group, that they would be faithful to set aside blocks of time for private prayer.
115. Pray for the people in the immediate "settings" of the group members—the "linked" people in their home/school/work environments.
116. Pray for God to speak to each person in the group individually about the use of "their" money.
117. Share recent experiences of successfully casting down sinful thoughts. (It's best to avoid going into too much detail about the sinful thoughts.)
118. Do you share the author's struggle with poor use of excessive amounts of free time?
119. Have you achieved a long-range goal in your life? What helped you to achieve it?
120. Have you spent your "down time" hanging out with God recently? Is this something you can share?
121. Pray for friends and loved ones, nameless if advisable, who are burrowing deeply into dark places and need to come out into the light of God.
122. What forms of recreation have you found to be refreshing and re-equipping?
123. Have members of the group experienced the truth of the lesson that there is nothing which cannot be forgiven?
124. Pray for Christians in prison for their faith, and for the prisoners' families.
125. How many hours do you give to the various news media on a weekly basis? Lift these hours up to God, and pray that God will direct each group member in reassessing that time.

126. Do you know Christians who probably "minister to God" regularly during church meetings?
127. Read Psalm 133. Pray to love God's huge plans more than your own ideas of how things "ought to be."
128. Pray for wisdom and boldness in speaking out to fellow Christians who are "playing with fire."
129. How can we avoid being too much like Julie (not her real name)?
130. Pray God's blessing on the other Christian churches in your area. Pray that leaders in the different churches would seek fellowship with each other.
131. Is there an arrow which God (quickly or finally) has pulled out of your soul?
132. What sins of others are the hardest for you to forgive? Is there anyone you are still refusing to forgive?
133. Have you experienced the problem of "disengaging" so as to focus on "God's manna for the new day"? What could you do differently next time?
134. Do you have any "memorials" of what God has done in your life? Have they helped you remember His goodness?
135. Share biographies or autobiographies which have inspired you in the areas of courage, faithfulness, or perseverance.
136. Are you discontented because of something God hasn't given you?
137. Have you ever found yourself attempting to minister to others while "running on fumes"?
138. In the months and years ahead, how will you remind yourself to drink, and drink, and drink again from the fountain of life?
139. What can happen when someone temporarily becomes the little god of his or her day?
140. When you wander off God's path, do you tend to jump right back on? How fast is your average turn-around time?
141. Have you found the promises of Isaiah 64:4-5 to be true?
142. Have you learned personally that "the backslider in heart will have his fill of his own ways"?

CPSIA information can be obtained at www.ICGtesting.com
Printed in the USA
BVOW02s1313120815

413069BV00001B/11/P